Building A New Tomorrow God's Way

*Love you Karen
May God's Truth be Yours!
Audrey Swanson*

Building A New Tomorrow God's Way

Audrey Swanson

Unless otherwise indicated, all Scripture quotations are taken from the New King James Version, Spirit Filled Bible, NKJV. Thomas Nelson Publishers.

Building A New Tomorrow God's Way
ISBN-13: 9781530022359
ISBN-10: 1530022355
Copyright 2016 by Audrey Swanson

Printed in the United States of America.
All rights reserved under international Copyright Law. Contents and/or cover may not be reproduced in whole or in part in any form without the express written consent from Audrey Swanson.

Acknowledgements

I am so blessed to have prayer partners in Minnesota and Arizona who care about me as a part of Jesus' family. They are true friends. Their prayers and encouragement have carried me through to the finished work of this book. Their Godly support has kept me writing! "Never stop," they would say, "on an assignment given by God." "Besides He will provide all you need to get it done." Thank you ladies!

Melany Messinger waded through the chapters and edited the book. Bless you Melany for your support of giving back to God what He has given you! Together we make a team to win this race to completion. We did it with God's grace and mercy.

God gave me friends to help me with the correct formatting and the actual finishing of my first book. Your work is so appreciated.

I speak a blessing of happiness and joy over you all as you continue to seek Him.

Foreword

This book is written to the Soul who is wondering what to do next, realizing this world and its people are falling apart, without mentioning names or political parties. I have nicknamed you "Same O." You realize people have become so self-centered, mean and ugly, that you think there seems to be no answer for any of it.

    I have written this book to tell you why there is such ugly evil "stuff" happening. I go farther and give you great clues on how you can maneuver through it all. If you mean "business" with God and desire a change in your life you will find answers here. Please keep on reading for I am praying that you will see the "impact" you can still have on your own life and others you love. If you recognize correction needed and make that correction, God promises you a happier and healthier life. Jesus still loves you no matter what is going on around you. Learn from this writing how God will help you find a way to live with joy and thus, you will be able to help others through their struggles, too!

Composed 6.01.12 – 4.25.14

Contents

	Acknowledgements · v
	Foreword · vii
Chapter 1	The Garden of Eden Story · 1
Chapter 2	Where did Satan Come From · · · · · · · · · · · · · · · · · 4
Chapter 3	Where Did Lucifer Come From · · · · · · · · · · · · · · · · 9
Chapter 4	Born Again Like Nick · 15
Chapter 5	Who I Am In Christ · 21
Chapter 6	Faith Triumphs · 33
Chapter 7	Love · 40
Chapter 8	Words · 45
Chapter 9	Keep Your Heart · 53
Chapter 10	Evolution · 60
Chapter 11	Body, Soul and Spirit · 65
Chapter 12	Mercy, Law and Grace · 70
Chapter 13	The Law · 77
Chapter 14	Atonement · 85
Chapter 15	Grace · 89
Chapter 16	Our Covenant · 96
Chapter 17	Prayer · 102
Chapter 18	Baptism in the Holy Spirit · · · · · · · · · · · · · · · · · 115
Chapter 19	The Sovereignty of God · · · · · · · · · · · · · · · · · · · 123

Chapter 20	Believers Have the Mind of Christ	129
Chapter 21	Money	133
Chapter 22	Healing	138
Chapter 23	Paul's Thorn	148
Chapter 24	Angels - Heaven's Host	152
Chapter 25	Abundant Life	160
Chapter 26	Trust Me	167
Chapter 27	Tell Them I Am Coming	170
	Endnotes	177

I
The Garden of Eden Story

Do you want a new beginning? Then you are reading the right book. With our Maker at our side we will pick up the pieces of yesterday and start building a new tomorrow. Did you know you are a triune being? You have a soul, which is your mind, will, and emotions, you live in a body and you are a spirit. God is a Spirit and we are a spirit. The way God communicates with you is spirit to spirit. The Bible says in 2 Corinthians 5:17 we are made brand new, we are a new creation a new species once we are walking with God. You ask, "How can I walk with God? I want more out of my life! I have heard a lot of sermons concerning God but nothing changes in my life. My life is still just the 'same o' 'same o'!" God's Kingdom is anything but the "same o" "same o". It is different from the natural world. The natural world is run by man operating in his five senses which are tasting, smelling, seeing, hearing, and feeling. God's Kingdom is run by Faith. Hebrews 11:1 and Hebrews 11:6 say. *"Now faith is the substance of things hoped for the evidence of things not seen. But, without faith it is impossible to please Him for he who comes to God must believe that He is, and that He is a rewarder of those who diligently seek Him."*

The natural man runs his life by his soul which is made up of his mind (reasoning), emotions, and his will and the body. These all rotate around the five senses. God's kingdom is ruled by faith. John 3:3 reads *"Verily, verily, I say unto thee, except a man be born again, he cannot see the kingdom of God"* KJV. You must place your faith in your Creator and what he has done for you. Let us read it in John 3:16-18 *"For God so loved the world that he gave his only begotten Son, that whosoever believes in him should not perish, but have everlasting life. For God sent not his Son into the world to condemn the world; but that the world through him might be saved. He that believes on him is not condemned: but he that believes not is condemned already, because he hath not believed in the name of the only begotten Son of God."* Have faith in the fact that God created you and loves you so much he died for you. John 15:9 reads *"As the Father has loved Me, so have I loved you: continue ye in my love."* KJV

Have you heard about the Garden of Eden story and how Adam and Eve were created? God really did all that as it is recorded in the creation story in Genesis. Really! He spoke and there it was! He actually created the heavens and earth and all that is tangibly seen before he created Adam of the dust of the ground, and breathed life into him! Did you catch that - LIFE!? Genesis 2:7 says, *"And the Lord God formed man of the dust of the ground, and breathed into his nostrils the breath of life: and man became a living soul."* KJV This life was God's life that was breathed into him. When Adam was first created he had six senses. Adam and Eve were totally naked and they did not have a clue as to what today's mankind thinks of as nakedness. Before the FALL (Genesis 2:1-25) in the garden of Eden there was no: fear, anxiety, lust, weeds, discouragement, anger, depression, downers or uppers, sadness, disease, sickness, poverty, and all that negativity. "Same O" do you know why that was so? Those negativities did not exist!! It was not until Adam committed high treason and Eve was deceived that God's universe started to fall apart and deteriorate! In the book 'You've Already Got It' the author writes, "Satan lied to them by saying. 'You don't have it all. As good as this is, there's more!' The truth is, they had it all. But the devil enticed them to speculate about what might be, would be or could be in Genesis 3:6. Through that, he caused perfect people living perfect lives in a perfect place to FALL. Adam and Eve threw it all away because a talking snake convinced them they didn't have enough."[1] Doesn't that scenario make a fantastic fairy tale? WRONG! It is the truth! That scenario is what happened some six thousand years back in time. Let's not back up in time let us catch up and think about the future to come.

APPLICATION

We communicate to God in our sixth sense. That is our faith.
Faith is the foundational block for a better tomorrow.
The Garden of Eden was a real place.
Living long ago, Adam and Eve were real people.
Hebrews 11:1 says "Now faith is the substance of things hoped for, the evidence of things not seen."
Hebrews 11:6 says "But without faith it is impossible to please Him, for he who comes to God must believe that He is, and that He is a rewarder of those who diligently seek Him."
Are you diligently seeking HIM? Then things will change.

II
Where did Satan Come From

Did you ever wonder where Satan came from? I have wondered about this. Especially since we know God is good all the time. John 10:10 says *"The thief does not come except to steal, and to kill, and to destroy. I have come that they may have life, and that they may have it more abundantly."* "Same O", have you ever wondered why God would create someone to torment the humans he loved and had said about them "It is good." We read in Genesis. 1:31, *"And God saw everything that he had made, and indeed, it was very good..."* "Same O" I learned about a loving heavenly Father who is a triune God. He is one, yet He is made up of three: God the Father, God the Son and God the Holy Spirit. Genesis 1:1-3 states *"In the beginning God created the heaven and the earth. And the earth was without form, and void; and darkness was upon the face of the deep. And the Spirit of God moved upon the face of the waters. And God said, Let there be light: and there was light."* I heard it said this way: that in eons of time "back in time: God the Father, who is the Alpha and the Omega (Rev. 1:8), called a meeting in the time of space in the heavenlies. Around this conference table of love sat: God the Father, God the Son and God the Holy Spirit. I heard them talking about the fact their hearts are so full of love they need a family to love. God asked at the table who will go and solve the sin issue into which man will FALL? This issue was solved by LOVE himself. Jesus raised his hand and said 'I will go Father.' 'Father I will go and do your will not mine'."

Why do I know it is all about love? Because the printed word says God is Love? 1 John 4:8 says, *"He who does not love does not know God, for God is love."* You know what "Same O", because God is omnipresent (everywhere present), omniscient (all knowing) and omnipotent (all powerful) we find God solving a mankind issue before man is created. Yes, God knows everything. Jeremiah 23:23-24 says *"Am I a God near at hand, says the Lord. And not a God afar off? Can anyone hide himself in secret places, so I shall not see him? Says the LORD. Do not I fill heaven and earth? says the LORD."* So why even try to argue with him or hide anything from him? He will just love you. You and I have the ability to love with our attitude. God's love far exceeds that! He is the essence of Love itself. Back to the conference table. Matthew 26:42 states, *"...O my Father, if this cup cannot pass away from Me, unless I drink it, Your will be done."* Jesus always did the Father's will. He was ready to be incarnated for all mankind, because of His love.

Referring back to chapter one what has now happened concerning Adam and Eve's free will. I see Adam and Eve in the Garden of Eden trying to cover themselves with fig leaves. Genesis 3:7 says *"Then the eyes of them both were opened, and they knew that they were naked; and they sewed fig leaves together, and made themselves coverings."* Oh oh, something has happened! What change has taken place from the previous chapter to now? I said they did not know they were naked. Their eyes where opened. What does that mean for Adam and Eve? Their physical eyes were able to see the giraffes, birds, lions, kittens and flowers etc. All those tangible articles (creation itself) they could see clearly. Now their spiritual eyes <u>lost</u> their sixth sense of faith and have opened up the door to see though a dark side of life that had never existed until the FALL. Adam and Eve the parents of all mankind became afraid! Genesis 3:10 says *"...I heard your voice in the garden and I was afraid because I was naked and I hid myself."*

Well, where did this Satan come from anyway? Why was he so mean too Adam and Eve? Or was he trying to be mean, ugly, and evil towards God? Satan knew God loved Adam and Eve. Satan's first name was Lucifer and he was a part of God's inner circle of three angels that worked for God in heaven. Lucifer was one of God's most prominent angels in heaven. Lucifer, was the archangel that praised God with all that he had and directed all of heaven to praise and honor God. He did this until he wanted what God had. Satan wanted to be God. Isaiah 14:12-14 says, *"How you are fallen from heaven, O Lucifer, son of the morning, how you are cut down to the ground, You which weakened the nations! For you have said in thine heart, I will ascend into heaven, I will exalt my throne above the stars of God: I will sit also upon the mount of the congregation, on the farthest sides of the north: I will ascend above the heights of the clouds; I will be like the Most High."* Pride always comes before a fall according to Proverbs 16:18 which reads *"Pride goes before destruction, and a haughty spirit before a fall."* He was "the music leader" of heaven until he decided he wanted more (Ezekiel 28:13:15).

I want to introduce you to two more archangels who are of great importance to God. Before we move to chapter three and find out how and why Lucifer became Satan. I want to share that these angels were and still are named, Gabriel and Michael. We hear about Gabriel in the Christmas story. Do you remember the angel that came before Zechariah while he was executing the priest's office? Gabriel showed up there because he is the archangel that brings messages to people under God's direction. Read it all in Luke 1:1-80. It is a beautiful rendition of LOVE, compassion and direction on God's part and great faith and obedience on the part of all the people in that one chapter. Look at the depth of Love in that story, it is TRUTH and it will give you goose bumps. We are not looking for goose bumps though, are we "Same O", but rather for something that can change your life to make it better. Please keep reading.

The other archangel, Michael you will meet as a warrior in the story of Daniel. Gabriel showed up here also, and makes an announcement to Daniel in answer to his prayer in Daniel 9:20-22. It states, *"Now while I was speaking, praying, and confessing my sin and the sin of my people Israel, and presenting my supplication before the Lord my God for the holy mountain of my God; Yes, while I was speaking in prayer, the man Gabriel, whom I had seen in the vision at the beginning, being caused to fly swiftly, reached me about the time of the evening offering. And he informed and talked with me, and said, 'O Daniel, I am now come forth to give thee skill to understand'.*" That prayer took him about three minutes to pray and his answer manifested almost immediately. Notice in Daniel 9:23 "*At the beginning of thy supplications the command went out, and I have come to tell you, for you are greatly beloved: therefore consider the matter, and understand the vision*". God moved in the spiritual world and gave the command at the very beginning of Daniel's prayer, yet it took approximately three minutes for Gabriel to show up, This is taken from the book "You've Already Got it!"[1] Daniel prayed again in chapter ten with very different results. In Daniel 10:12 God says "*your words were heard, and I have come because of your words.*" Gabriel said "*But the prince of the kingdom of Persia* (a demonic Power) *withstood me one and twenty days (three weeks): and behold, Michael, one of the chief princes* (another angel see Jude 9 and Revelation 12:17*), came to help me; for I had been left alone there with the kings of Persia.*" It took weeks of help from Michael to break through the demonic opposition and manifest Daniel's answer! There was and still is demonic opposition. So from this standpoint let us check out the truth about Lucifer in the next chapter.

APPLICATION

Do not give up in prayer.
When your heart is right and you seek God for help, remember
He heard you when you prayed.
Your prayer was answered when you prayed.
Between the amen and the manifestation of the prayer
did you persevere or did you give up?
Daniel did not give up!!!
Did you pray a selfish prayer?
A selfish prayer is one that does not line up with the word of God.
When your prayer does not line up with the word of God your motive is wrong, so check up on your heart attitude.
Ask the Lord to show you where you missed it, receive His instruction and change when He tells you where to change.
That will take you out of the "same o" "same o" status in which you find yourself, "Same O".

III
Where Did Lucifer Come From

God created by WORDS. Look in Genesis' chapter one and see all the "Then God said," lines. It means just that; God said it, and it was so (CREATED). In Psalms 89:34 we find, *"My covenant I will not break, nor alter the word that is gone out of my lips"*. When God says something it is a covenant out of His mouth. Notice in Hebrews 1:2-3, *"God has in these last days spoken unto us by his Son, whom he hath appointed heir of all things, through whom also He made the worlds; who being the brightness of his glory, and the express image of His person, and upholding all things by the word of His power, when he had by Himself purged our sins, sat down on the right hand of the Majesty on high."* If God would break His word we would self-destruct! Genesis 1:26 says we are created in His image. It is recorded in Genesis 1:28, *"Then God blessed them, and God said unto them, be fruitful, and multiply, and fill the earth, and subdue it: and have dominion over the fish of the sea, and over the fowl of the air, and over every living thing that moves upon the earth."* So "Same O" be fruitful - and have dominion!

Man has dominion over this earth not God. God gave mankind authority over the earth. In Psalm 82:6 we read, *"I said, you are gods; and all of you are children of the Most High."* See -'YOU are gods' a 'god' over the earth. <u>You are Not Divinity!</u> We had the *dominion* and we caused the transgression by giving to Satan what God had given mankind. God as a Spirit had to become a man in order to take back from Satan that which man gave him. When did man give to Satan what God gave to him? It was when Adam and Eve ate the fruit of the tree of good and evil. Genesis 2:17 says, "*But of the tree of the knowledge of good and evil, you shall not eat: for in the day that you eat of it you shall surely die.*" John 1:3 states, "*All things were made through Him; and without Him nothing was made that was made.*" If we were God we would say, "Throw them all out and do it over." God does not break any of His covenants! Satan now uses the power and authority God gave mankind. He cannot do anything without man's cooperation! Romans 5:12 says, "*Therefore, just as through one man sin entered into the world, and death through sin; and thus death spread to all men, because all sinned.*" Death came as a result of Adams sin. Death came through Adam. It did not happen before him. Mankind empowered the devil.

Christians must resist the devil. The devil <u>flees</u> from <u>you</u>. You cannot ask or beg God to get rid of him in prayer. You have been given the authority so you must use it. God cannot. Yes, "Same O", I meant God cannot. Jesus won that conflict between Himself and Satan. This happened when he died on the cross and went to hell to get the Keys of Death in Hades. Revelation 1:18 says, "*I am He who lives, and was dead; and, behold, I am alive forevermore, Amen; and I have the keys of Hades (hell) and of death...*" I have heard it said this way "Same O" that Satan is nothing but a zero with the rim knocked off. Stop magnifying the devil. The body of Christ is often used by Satan. Unbelievers are used by Satan. The truth is that people all around the world today are being influenced, controlled, and used --- to varying degrees --- by the devil. Remember Satan is defeated. As a born again Christian <u>you have authority over him</u>. Satan is not using some super human authority and power given to him by God. He got his authority from mankind.

Satan was <u>not</u> placed in the Garden of Eden to tempt Adam. God placed Lucifer there to minister to Adam and Eve. Lucifer was to encourage them. How did Lucifer become Satan? Remember Lucifer was the worship leader of Heaven! Lucifer had pipes and instruments built in his being. Ezekiel 28:13 says, "*Thou has been in Eden the garden of God: every precious stone was your covering, the sardius, topaz, and the diamond, the beryl, the onyx, and the jasper, the sapphire, turquoise, and emerald, and the carbuncle, and gold: the workmanship of thy tabrets (tumbrels) and of thy pipes was prepared in thee in the day that you were created. Thou art thee anointed cherub ... KJV."* He was not a tiny cute baby cherubim. Cherubs are POWERFUL! Remember "Same O" because of pride Lucifer's goal was to become God. So how could Lucifer overcome God? He could not!!!! Lucifer wanted to overrule God. Lucifer used Adam and Eve as hostages to attack God and take from God. He could only do this as Adam and Eve <u>willingly obeyed</u> Lucifer. Rom.6:16 says, *"Do you not know that to whom you present yourselves slaves to obey, you are the one's slaves whom you obey, whether of sin leading to death or of obedience leading to righteousness?"* He got man to yield to him. MAN - the instance man took and ate the fruit - man gave all his power to Lucifer. Then Adam and Eve became hostage to Lucifer because they yielded to him. This "being" became Satan when Adam transgressed.

Adam had, total dominion over the earth and this title deed was transferred to the devil. Satan does not have some great super angelic power to rule. He is using man's power that God gave Adam and Eve. Because Satan is a spirit he had to use Adam, a human being to do something here on earth. Because God is a spirit he had to use a human being, Jesus, to do something here on this earth Spirits need a body in order to operate here on this earth. Jesus knew full well why he was going to come to earth. It was to take back for mankind what man had given to the evil one, namely Satan. Jesus paid the price in full with his life. First Corinthians 6:20 is as follows; *"For you were bought with a price: therefore glorify God in your body, and in your spirit, which are God's."*

Ephesians 6:10 talks about the wiles of the devil. All Satan can do is to deceive you and me and get us to believe a lie. Satan can speak things into our heads. But for a born again believer we know the birds can fly over us but <u>by our authority</u> "in Christ" we can pull down every evil imagination! 2 Corinthians 10:4-5 says, *"For the weapons of our warfare are not carnal, but mighty in God for pulling down strongholds; casting down arguments (imaginations) and every high thing that exalts itself against the knowledge of God, bringing every thought into captivity to the obedience of Christ.*" Satan cannot make you depressed, sick, poor, etc. unless you submit and are deceived like Adam and Eve. Stop cooperating with Satan, and then he is dead in the water. God did not create this supernatural being to come down and beat up everybody. Lucifer rebelled at God through deceiving mankind. WE empowered Satan and he cannot do anything without our consent or cooperation. Who created Satan then? If God had "taken out" Satan at the very beginning in the garden he would have had to "take out" Adam and Eve too! God kept his covenant. He always keeps His word. WE created Satan. That 'Being' was Lucifer. But, the very moment Adam ate of the fruit of the tree he became Satan. Mankind did it.

Dare you think this too is a fairy tale, it is not! Believe me, "Same O" it is not. Remember the Holy Bible is the only anchor we have in this day. We can hang our life on this anchor of Truth. Satan is using mankind's authority and power to steal, kill and destroy. We must use the authority God gave back to us through the death, burial, and resurrection of Jesus Christ when He said in Mathew 28: 18-20 KJV, "..*.All power is given unto me (Jesus) in heaven and in earth. Go therefore, and teach all nations, baptizing them in the name of the Father, and of the Son, and of the Holy Ghost: Teaching them to observe all things whatsoever I have commanded you: and lo, I am with you always, even unto the end of the world.*" Mark 16:15-18 KJV further instructs us to "*Go ye into all the world, and preach the gospel to every creature. He that beliveth and is baptized shall be saved; but he that believeth not shall be damned. And these signs shall follow them that believe; in my name shall they cast out devils; they shall speak with new tongues; they shall take up serpents; and if they drink any deadly thing, it shall not hurt them; they shall lay hands on the sick, and they shall recover.*"

"Same O", the first step in walking correctly into God's Kingdom and seeing a change in your life, is to believe what the Word says about Jesus, to believe the WORD for face value, and do what it tells you to do. You see, to use the authority that is available to you, you must be born again, because that authority comes only through the name of Jesus. "Same O" that is the first step! So part of your "same o" "same o" problem is the fact you cannot use the weapons given to you by the resurrected Jesus IF you are not born again. In the next chapter I will show you how easy it is to become a true Christian. This will cut a big hole in the "same o" "same o" life you want to change. Let us look forward to a better life in Christ by applying the things we learn.

APPLICATION

Remember Satan is defeated. Jesus defeated him. Satan works on your brain to mess you up and to do his bidding and make God look like a liar.

Paul warns of false leaders in 2 Corinthians 11:3 *"But I fear, lest by any means, as the serpent beguiled Eve through his subtilty, so your minds should be corrupted from the simplicity that is in Christ." KJV*

Remember music and praise is a weapon the devil has <u>no defense against</u>. God inhabits the praises of his people. Psalm 22:3 *"But thou are holy, O thou that inhabitest the praises of thy people." KJV*

Adam caused the FALL in the Garden for all mankind. JESUS caused the VICTORY on the CROSS for all mankind. That victory is yours and mine by our <u>choice</u>. Acts 4:12 says, *"Neither is there salvation in any other: for there is none other name under heaven given among men, whereby we must be saved." KJV*

"Same O", I am believing that you will know Jesus not only as your Savior, who will redeem you from hell, but also know him as your Lord (and learn what is yours in Christ Jesus) by the time you get to the end of this book. If Jesus is your Lord, your life **will** change.

IV
Born Again Like Nick

Now that we know who Lucifer was and where Satan came from, let us look at the fact that God did not create such a beautiful world to let mankind wonder if they can make it to heaven. Why would God do that? That would be mean, if you ask me. We have previously established that God is always good, Psalm 145:8-9. Satan loves to hinder people from coming to the Lord, remember, his only "power" is fear, deception and lies. The devil cannot keep you from doing anything. If he could, he would keep you from being born again. You may be the worst selfish person, dope addict, or mean person on the face of the earth; yet in any dismal state, you can call out and receive the greatest miracle of all, a new birth. Or you can be the holiest person by actions and still need a new birth, so you too must call out for salvation. Why? Because even though Jesus died for you 2000 years ago, as Romans 3:23 says, *"For all have sinned and fall short of the glory of God."* you must believe and repent to be born-again.

Adam and Eve sinned and their spirit man died to God and they lost their communion with God and became united with the devil. (It's the 'evil one' who tempts us to sin.) They then became by nature a child of wrath, a child of the devil. So that makes us (mankind) born with a sin <u>nature</u>. Remember it is not the things you do that make you a sinner it is the sin nature that makes you do the things you do. It is not a matter of changing your behavior. It is a fact you are by nature a sinner. You can change this sin nature by believing His Word.

Salvation is coming to the Lord and believing and having faith that when you pray and repent of your sin and make Jesus your Lord, you get born from above. Your actions change in accordance with who you are now - a child of God. You must be born from above or you will split hell wide open, even if you live a relatively holy life. You can't change the fact that Romans 3:23 says *"All have sinned and fall short of the glory of God"*. The verse that helped me to receive the truth of the scriptures was Romans 5:8 *"But God commendeth his love toward me, in that while I was yet a sinner Christ died for me."* KJV I knew from that verse I did not have to "clean up" first to come to God. God would listen to me just the way I was. That one week I attended the KYB (Kids and Youth Bible School) I had to make a decision. I knew at age eight, "Same O", God was wooing me. And every day I put Him off His wooing became weaker. That did frighten me! I was going to first pray my sin away and then come to God clean; then it dawned on me, there is no other God worth praying to!!

Do you know what Nicodemus did? Look him up in John chapter three where Jesus talks about the two births. In Jesus time Nicodemus, a Pharisee and a ruler of the Jews, wanted to know how to get to heaven. Being afraid of people and of his peers he went to Jesus secretly in the night to ask him personally how a man can be born again. So you see you are in good company. Like Nick you must also ask. Then turn to John chapter nineteen and read verses 31- 41. Nick understood and received his salvation because we find him at the cross helping Joseph of Arimathea take the body of Jesus off the cross. Once saved, you too, will find your love for Him makes it easy to serve Him.

"Same O", Jesus has done his part, and you are given a choice. You must choose. Your part is to believe Him and receive his free gift of salvation. Romans 10:9-10 states *"That if you confess with thy mouth the Lord Jesus, and believe in your heart that God has raised Him from the dead, you will be saved. For with the heart one believes unto righteousness; and with the mouth confession is made unto salvation."* Remember, demons also believe, as it says in James 2:19, *"the devils also believe and tremble"*. So the last part of the verse is important. Confession is made unto salvation, <u>believing with your heart</u> what Jesus did and then speaking and acting out what he has done for you. What has He done? We must start by believing the basics and grow from there.

I, by my choice make a decision through prayer to be saved.
Romans 10:9-10
He was born of a virgin. Matthew 1:20
He came as prophesied by the prophets. Matthew 1:22-23
He was born of an incorruptible seed. Matthew 1:18
He walked around on the face of the earth for about 33 and 1/3 years.
His ministry began after he received the power of the Holy Ghost.
Matthew 3:16-17, Acts 10:38
He preached, healed and taught the people the latter 3 and 1/3 years.
He was hated to the point they (man-with the sin nature)
crucified Him. Matthew 27:35
He "gave of" his life and died on the cross. Matthew 27:50
He was buried in a tomb with Pilate's seal of approval.
Matthew 27:66
He arose from the dead. Matthew 28:5-6
He sits at the right hand of God in Heaven, interceding for us.
Mark 16:19, Romans 8:27

<u>JESUS is the only man that shed his blood upon a cross, died and came back to life because of his love for you and me</u>.

In the Holy Bible KJV there is a list of "infallible proofs" <u>according to eye witnesses of his resurrection</u>. There is no doubt that He is for real. God does not lie. Numbers 23:19 says, *"is not a man, that he should lie; nor a son of man, that he should repent: Has he said, and will he God not do?"* Also read Titus 1:2, *"In hope of eternal life, which God, who cannot lie, promised before time….."* The above are basic scriptures which pictorially show Jesus' love for you. He loved you so much He gave his life for you so you could be a part of his family. You must choose Him. He does not force anybody to join His team or coerce anybody to do something for Him. He is a perfect gentlemen. The least we can do is believe Him and ask to receive <u>our free gift of salvation for now and eternity.</u>

Just Simply Pray.

God in heaven I believe your son Jesus died on the cross and He rose from the dead for me. I receive what He has done for me. I admit I am a sinner and I repent of my sin and the rejecting of you till now Jesus. I surrender my life to you to be my Lord. Thank you for this free gift of salvation. Please help me to live the rest of my life for you. Thank you for your love. I love you too! I receive my salvation by faith. I now know I am saved. I pray this in the name of Jesus. Amen.

Christ <u>only</u> dies for the <u>ungodly</u> as it says in Romans 5:6, *"Christ died for the ungodly"*...verse eight says, *"But, God commendeth his love toward us, in that, while we were yet sinners Christ died for us"*. Romans 8:9 says, *"Being now justified by his blood, we shall be saved from wrath through him."* *KJV*. Praise God for this anchor we have, the TRUTH of the Word. The bible is Jesus in print "Same O." First John 5:13-15 says, *"These things have I written to you that who believe in the name of the Son of God; that you may know that you have eternal life, and that you may continue to believe in the name of the Son of God. Now this is the confidence that we have in Him, that if we ask anything according to His will, He hears us: And if we know that He hears us, whatever we ask, we know that we have the petitions that we have asked of Him."* This tells me I can know, know that I know, I am going to heaven. If you prayed that prayer typed above and meant it, I will see you in heaven someday. Yes, you are now born again like Nicodemus. Praise the Lord!

The angels are rejoicing right along with me, because you chose to be born again. Luke 15:10 says, *"I say unto you, there is joy in the presence of the angels of God over one sinner that repents."* Remember this, if you were saved before you read this and are in the "same o" "same o" mode, keep reading. You will find some answers as you continue on. Let us pick up on WHO I AM IN CHRIST. That is, you now know, only for a born again believer. You are the new guy on the block, you are the new species.

The next chapter will definitely shed some light on you, the person that is stuck with the "same o" "same o" life that needs a new tomorrow built today!

APPLICATION

You must choose. Neither God nor Jesus will hit you over your head and say, "Do It Dummy." They do say,
"behold now is the accepted time; behold now is the day of salvation" that is in 2 Corinthians 6:2b KJV.
Remember what Romans 10:9 says, *"That if thou shall confess with thy mouth the Lord Jesus, and shalt believe in thine heart that God hath raised him from the dead, thou shalt be saved."*
You must move in the spirit realm when the Holy Spirit is wooing you. John 6:44 reads, *"No man can come to me, except the Father which hath sent me <u>draw him</u>: and I will raise him up at the last day."*
He is talking to you right now. Don't miss His open door!
Romans 10:13, "For whoever shall call upon the name of the Lord shall be saved."
Please listen to his wooing and pray the above simple prayer or a facsimile, from your heart.

V
Who I Am In Christ

HEY, HEY, IF - JUST IF you applied the last chapter to your life you now are on a brand new walk with Jesus. It is called the game of life. There are no reruns. It is living your **life in Christ Jesus.** We must play it having a winning attitude. Our faith in Him causes us to expect to win at the game of life. Most of us don't come by that attitude easily. We think about 'losing' or 'lack of' as our life rut. Our mind set needs to change "Same O." Thinking wrong keeps us in that "same o" "same o" rut. <u>Continuing</u> to think in that "same o" rut we will not see that change in our life we so desperately want. We will have to totally change our mindset to what God says about us. Let's develop a glorious sense of confidence that says, "Hey Devil, I am going to be victorious and there is not a thing you can do to stop me!" Well to think like that and act upon it correctly we must know who we are in Christ. First John 5:5 tells a born-again believer we have the right to be a winner, to overcome every aspect of this evil (note evil) world. It states, *"Who is he who overcomes the world, but he who believes that Jesus is the Son of God?"* To you "Same O" as the new one born from above and the "oldie" who has stood with Christ for years, we will all find this review of "WHO I AM IN CHRIST" very refreshing. There is not a known author[1] for this particular list, except we know the author of the scriptures is the Holy Spirit Himself (2 Timothy 3:16). As we read it and meditate on it, the newness of the Word of Life, coupled with our faith, <u>will</u> encourage each of us.

21

I AM GOD'S CHILD because I AM born again, not of a perishable seed, but of imperishable, through the living and enduring word of God. 1 Peter 1:23

I AM BORN AGAIN through the word of truth to be a firstfruit of all he created. James 1:18

I AM ADOPTED as God's son through Jesus Christ. Ephesians 1:5

I AM FORGIVEN of all my sins on account of His name. 1 John 2:12

I AM PURIFIED from <u>all</u> <u>unrighteousness</u> because I have confessed my sins. 1 John 1:9

I AM REDEEMED from the <u>Empty</u> <u>Way</u> of life handed down to me by my forefathers. I Peter 1:18-19

I AM REDEEMED from the curse of the law. Galatians 3:13

I AM REDEEMED through His blood by the riches of God's grace. Ephesians 1:7

I AM CLEANSED IN MY CONSCIENCE with the blood of Christ. Hebrews 9:14

I AM A SERVANT of the living God! Hebrews 9:14

I AM A NEW CREATION, the old has gone, the new has come! 2 Corinthians 5:17

I AM A TEMPLE OF THE HOLY SPIRIT who is in me. 1 Corinthians 6:19

I AM RESCUED from the dominion of darkness and

I AM DELIVERED into the kingdom of the Son.
Colossians 1:13

I AM BLESSED with every spiritual blessing in Christ.
Ephesians 1:3

I AM BLESSED through my faith. Deuteronomy 28:1-14

I AM OVERTAKEN with **BLESSINGS**. Deuteronomy 28:1-14

I AM GRANTED PROSPERITY as I fully obey the Lord my God; in my city & country, in my family, in my work, in my coming and going, before my enemies. Deuteronomy 28:1-14

I AM ESTABLISHED as his holy people.
Deuteronomy 28:1-14

I AM A LENDER to many and borrower from none.
Deuteronomy 28:1-14

I AM THE HEAD and not the tail. Deuteronomy 28:1-14

I AM ALWAYS AT THE TOP, never at the bottom.
Deuteronomy 28:1-14, Galatians 3:9

I AM CHOSEN by God to be holy and dearly loved,
Colossians 3:12 since before the beginning of time.
1 Timothy 1:9, 1 Thessalonians 1:4, Ephesians. 1:4

I AM HOLY and **BLAMELESS** in his sight. Ephesians 1:4

I AM KEPT STRONG to the end. 1 Corinthians 1:8

I AM BROUGHT NEAR through the blood of Christ, I who was once far away. Ephesians 2:13

I AM AN HEIR to everything new and the spring of the water of life. Revelation. 21:5-7

I AM SET FREE by the truth. John 8:31-32

I AM STRONG in the Lord and in his mighty power. Ephesians 6:10

I AM DEAD to **Sin:** Romans 8:2

I AM DEAD to the **Basic Principals of this world;** Colossians 2:20

I AM SAVED by God's Free Grace. Ephesians: 5, 8 & 9

I AM CRUCIFIED with Christ. I no longer live, but Christ lives in me. Galatians 2:20

I AM ALIVE in GOD in Jesus Christ. Romans 6:11

I AM FREE of any CONDEMNATION. Romans 8:1

I AM HEALED by his wounds. 1 Peter 2:24, Isaiah 53:5

I AM A CO-HEIR WITH CHRIST in his sufferings & his glory. Romans 8:17

I AM A SHAREHOLDER in the inheritance of the saints in the kingdom of light. Colossians 1:12

I AM A CITIZEN with God's People and a member of God's household. Ephesians 2:19

I AM MORE THAN A CONQUEROR through him who loved me. Romans 8:37

I AM ONE WHO HAS my **MIND SET** on what the Spirit desires. My mind is controlled by the Spirit and is life and peace. Romans 8:5-6

I AM IN Christ Jesus. I have his wisdom from God-that is, my righteousness, holiness & redemption. 1 Corinthians 1:30

I AM LAVISHED with all WISDOM and UNDERSTANDING and the mystery of his will. Ephesians1:8

I AM RECONCILED to God through Christ. 2 Corinthians 5:18

I AM A MINISTER of RECONCILIATION. 2 Corinthians 5:18

I AM ROOTED & BUILT UP in him, strengthened in my faith. Colossians 2:7

I AM OVERFLOWING with thankfulness. Colossians 2:7

I AM CIRCUMCISED not with a circumcision done by the hands of men but with the circumcision done by Christ. Colossians 2:11

I AM SOLIDLY BUILT ON THE FOUNDATION of the apostles and prophets, with Christ Jesus himself as the chief cornerstone. Ephesians 2:20

I AM FREE OF FEAR in love. I love because Jesus first loved me. 1 John 4:18-19

I AM KEPT SAFE from the evil one. Satan cannot harm me. 1 John 5:18

I AM HIS CHOSEN and **FAITHFUL FOLLOWER**. Revelation 17:14b

I AM GOD'S DEARLY LOVED CHILD Ephesians 5:1

I AM LOVED by God. John 13:34, Colossians. 3:12, 1 Thessalonians 1:4

I AM THE SALT of the earth. Matthew 5:13

I AM THE LIGHT of the world. Matthew 5:14

I AM THE RIGHTEOUSNESS OF GOD in Jesus. 2 Corinthians 5:21, 1 Peter 2:24

I AM A PARTICIPANT in the divine nature through his very great and precious promises, escaping the corruption in the world caused by evil desires. 2 Peter 1:4

I AM GIFTED WITH SPIRITUAL GIFTS for the common good of the Body of Christ. 1 Corinthians 12:7, Ephesians 4:8, Romans 12:8

I AM A ROYAL PRIESTHOOD, a holy nation, a person belonging to God, and

I AM CALLED OUT OF DARKNESS into his wonderful light that I may declare the praises of him. 1 Peter 2:9

I AM CHRIST'S AMBASSADOR 2 Corinthians 5:20

I AM NOT ASHAMED OF THE GOSPEL, because it is the power of God for the salvation of everyone who believes.
Romans 1:16

I AM AS BOLD AS A LION. Proverbs 28:1

I AM GOD'S WORKMANSHIP to do good works, prepared in advance for me to do. Ephesians 2:10

I AM the **APPLE OF MY FATHER'S EYE**
Deuteronomy 32:10, Psalm 17:8

I AM HIDDEN in the shadow of his wings. Psalm 17:8

I AM BEING CHANGED into Christ's image.
Philippians 1:6, Col. 2:12

I AM RAISED UP with Christ
                    and
I AM SEATED with God in the heavenly realms in Christ Jesus.
Ephesians 2:8

I AM ONE with God and Jesus. John 17:21-23

I AM SET FREE from the law of sin and death to live by the law of the SPIRIT OF LIFE. Romans 8:2

I HAVE THE LORD'S BENEFITS
He forgives all my sins. He heals all my diseases.
He redeems my life from the pit. He crowns me with love and compassion
He satisfies my desires with good things. He renews my youth like the eagles.
He works righteousness & justice when I'm oppressed.
Psalms 103:3-4

I HAVE THE MIND of Christ. 1 Corinthians 2:16, Philippians 2:5

I HAVE AN INHERITANCE. Ephesians 1:11

I HAVE ACCESS by one Spirit to God the Father. Hebrews 4:16, Ephesians 2:18

I HAVE VICTORY over the world. 1 John 5:4

I HAVE EVERLASTING LIFE and will not be condemned.
and
I HAVE CROSSED OVER from death to life. John 5:24, John 6:47

I HAVE the **PEACE OF GOD** which transcends all under- standing. My heart and mind are guarded in Christ Jesus. Philippians 4:7

I HAVE RECEIVED POWER from the Holy Spirit to place my hands on sick people and they will get well; and to overcome all the power of the enemy; nothing will harm me.
Mark 16:16-18, Luke 10:17-19

MY LIFE IS HIDDEN with Christ in God. Colossians 3:3

I LIVE IN Christ Jesus. Colossians 2:6

I CAN DO EVERYTHING through Jesus who gives me strength. Philippians 4:13

I SHALL DO even greater works than Jesus Christ. John 14:12

I POSSESS THE GREATER ONE because greater is he who is in me than he who is in the world. 1 John 4:4

I PRESS ON toward the goal of a heavenly calling. Philippians. 3:14

I FIX MY EYES upon Jesus. Hebrews 12:2

I ALWAYS TRIUMPH in Christ and spread everywhere the fragrance of the knowledge of him. 2 Corinthians 2:14

I DECLARE his praises. 1 Peter 2:9

These scriptures are just a beginning of the truths that are ours **in Christ Jesus**.[1] To the degree we believe them and receive them as our very own determines the extent of the promises that will manifest in our lives. We are to be overcomers and have these victories happen. Some people say, "Oh, I am predestined to be this way", which is usually far below the victory walk. They say God predestined them to be in this low walk. That is another lie from Satan. God knows what you are going to do before you do it that is His definition of predestination. He did not predestine you to do it that way. God does not predetermine you to a low life. Romans 8:29-39 tells it all. Please take time to read that entire passage. *"For whom He foreknew, He also **predestined to be conformed to the image of His Son**, that he might be the firstborn among many brethren. Moreover whom He predestined, these He also called; whom He called, these He also justified; and whom He justified, these He also glorified. ....If God is for us, who can be against us? Romans 8: 29-31."*

WE MUST DEVELOP A WINNING ATTITUDE!
All those scriptures listed are LIFE. They are not just another story book to read. Receive these scriptures as truth, spoken straight from

the Father's mouth directly to you. If you apply them to your life, your life will be better.

Pondering the fact that we are created in God's image I must consider the fact we are a three-part being. We are made up of a body, soul and spirit. It was in our spirit that we were made perfect or born-again. Therefore, <u>we have all of God in our spirit</u>. Let us remember we have "it all - the fullness of God" in our spirit. What do I mean by "it all"? I am thinking about the fact when I was born again the Spirit of Truth came into me. Therefore I knew I was "in Christ" and "He is in me". Do you remember when Adam was made from the dust of the earth, and God breathed into him and he became alive? All of God is in this man Adam. When we became born again we received in us that same SPIRIT God first breathed in Adam. Think about this. This is the same God that created the universe. We have "all of God in us" just like Adam had "all of God in him" in the very beginning of his creation. Our problem is most born again believers do not know that. I hate to use the term Christian here because so many people think they are Christians by performance and not by the blood of the lamb shed on the cross. Jesus redeems us by his death and resurrection not by any of our works. In John 14:6 we find Jesus saying, *"I am the way, the truth, and the life. No one comes to the Father except through Me."* You do not add works of any kind whether your mind goes to more prayers, baptism, the Lords Supper or attendance in a church etc. <u>It is a gift.</u> All we do is ask of Him, believe Him, receive Him and confess Him as Savior and Lord and that is our **FREE GIFT.**

Now that we have "it all" we shall learn to walk in His commandments. Romans 10:4 says, *"For Christ is the end of the law."* 1 John 2:3 says, *"Now by this we know that we know Him, if we keep His commandments."* What is that? It is LOVE. Mathew 22: 37-38 says, *"...You shall love the Lord your God with all your heart, with all your soul, and with all your mind. This is the first and great commandment. And the second is like it: you shall love your neighbor as yourself.'"* This great commandment is ours to follow as we live in the era of Grace. As you walk out the Great Commandment you automatically fulfill the Ten Commandments. Isn't that neat "Same O"?

So don't think you have thrown out the Ten Commandments. We must learn to walk in love to fulfill our destiny in Christ. We cannot expect to receive much from God without walking in love. Why? Because *"Faith works through love."* Galatians 5:6. We cannot please God without <u>faith.</u> Hebrews 11:6 says, *"But without faith it is impossible to please him..."* If we are looking for a better tomorrow we had better take an aerial view of our life and notice what pleases the one that created us. LOVE and FAITH are essential factors that must be developed in our walk "in Christ". If anybody could help us it should be the one who put us together. He has the manual. Today that manual is printed out for us and it is called the Holy Bible. We must read it, meditate on it, and develop our relationship with our Redeemer and Savior. My Bible says in the footnotes: Just as salvation is appropriated by heart belief and spoken confession, so His continuing working in our lives is advanced by the same means. Beginning in this spirit of <u>saving</u> faith, let us grow in <u>active</u> faith–believing in God's mighty power for all our needs, speaking with our lips what our hearts receive and believe of the many promises in His Word. Let us accept God's "contracts" for all our need by endowing them with our confessed belief-just as when we were saved. (Acts 4:33, 1 Corinthians 11:23-26)

APPLICATION

Believe and Receive

Renew your mind by meditating on the verses of "Who I Am In Christ". Ask your Lord to reveal to you any ungodly beliefs your life is tangled around, repent, and rebuke that stronghold and lay hold to a new life in that area of your **life in Christ**. We may discover the ungodly beliefs one step at a time. Do not become dismayed, keep pursuing Truth and you will learn where you are performing and believing ungodly lies.

Performance is not <u>faith</u>, it is of the law. In fact performance nullifies your faith making it impossible for promises to manifest.

This "Same O" is one big reason some Believers are losing out on receiving what is rightfully theirs.

Romans 4:14 says, *"For if those who are of the law are heirs, faith is made void, and the promise made of no effect:"*

John 14:21 says, *"He who has My commandments and keeps them, it is he who loves Me. And he who loves Me will be loved by my Father, and I will love him and manifest Myself to him."*

Believe you are royalty.

Think about what that entails. You are a child of the King of kings.

1 Peter 2:9 says, *"But you are a chosen generation, a royal priesthood, a holy nation, His own special people, that you may proclaim the praises of Him who called you out of darkness into His marvelous light."*

VI
Faith Triumphs

Matthew 4:4 says, *"Man cannot live by bread alone, but by every word that proceeds from the mouth of God."* If you just became a born-again believer as explained in the previous chapter entitled "Born Again like Nick," you automatically used your faith and as Colossians 1:13 says, *"You were delivered from the power of darkness and you were translated into the kingdom of His dear Son." "You now are born of God and have world overcoming faith residing on the inside of you. For greater is He that is in you than he that is in the world"* (1 John 5:4-5: 1 John 4:4). Mark 11:22 in the literal translation says, *"We have the God kind of faith or faith of God."* This is ours because we have accepted Him through repentance, believed in Him and confessed Him as our Lord. Romans 10:17 says, *"Faith cometh by hearing, and hearing by the Word of God."* Once you are born again God has given you "the measure of faith." That is found in Romans 12:3. It reads as *"...to think soberly, as God has dealt to each one the measure of faith." KJV.* It is equal to God's faith. It is His faith in us, and now we must learn how to use it. Just like we strengthen our muscles by exercise, we too must strengthen our faith by using it. Using it develops it. Any talent we have is improved and developed by practice. So it is with our faith. God has designed us in such a way, that the just shall live by faith. The entrance of the everlasting Word, the incorruptible seed into our heart, gives us the born again experience called salvation.

Once saved we find God has good things planned for us we are capable of receiving of Him. God can and does plan for you and me for we are now His children. We are capable of receiving and believing that all things are possible for us "in Christ Jesus!" You see nothing is impossible with God. All the impossibility is with us when we measure God by our own limitations and unbelief!

Once we are "born again" we have all that Adam started out with before the "Fall." We have all of God in us now and we can grow up in Christ. God wants us to grow up in the knowledge of Him by using our faith. 1 Corinthians 2:1 says, *"I have fed you with milk and not with meat … you were unable to bear it…"* We now must change our natural mind, or carnal mind because it hinders our spiritual growth. How do we do that? We meditate on His Word. Hebrews 4:12 says, *"the Word of God is a living and **powerful** (life force), and sharper than any two edged sword, piercing even to the division of soul and spirit and of joints and marrow and is a discerner of the thoughts and intents of the heart."* This scripture is telling us that we are a three-part being. We are just that; a spirit, a soul (mind, will and emotions) and a body. It is also saying the scriptures divided correctly can help us with any problem we have in life. Through faith your spirit gets saved. Through faith you renew your mind (that is working on your soul) to the things you already have in your "spirit." You can learn to live successfully now, on this planet. Romans 12:1-2 tells us to be a living sacrifice to God. *"I beseech you therefore brethren, by the mercies of God that you present your bodies a living sacrifice, holy, acceptable to God, which is your reasonable service. And do not be conformed to this world, but be transformed by the renewing of your mind, that you may prove what is that good and acceptable and perfect will of God."* We do all this by believing we can trust God because we have faith in Him and the fact we now have His kind of faith working in us. We must put it into action. When you get your soul to agree with your spirit, you will find your body will follow in obedience to your heart of faith.

By faith we understand Hebrews 11:1 says, *"Now faith is the substance of things hoped for, the evidence of things not seen."* It also says in Hebrews 11:6, *"But, without faith it is impossible to please Him, for he who comes to God must believe that He is, and that He is a rewarder of those who diligently seek Him."* To have a successful life we must desire to please Him and walk the walk of

Building A New Tomorrow God's Way

faith. Let us not stop growing once in the door of salvation, let us thirst for more of God.

Let us look at Noah. "Same O" do you know the story of the man Noah? He walked on this earth many, many centuries back in time. In fact *"but Noah"*, the bible says *"found grace in the eyes of the Lord."* (Genesis 6:8) Hebrews 11:7 says, *"by faith Noah being divinely warned of things not yet seen, moved with godly fear, prepared an ark for the saving of his household, by which he condemned the world and became heir of the righteousness which is according to faith."* If you study his story in Genesis you will see the whole world was corrupt and going to hell in a 'hand bag.' God saw one righteous man that believed Him and we see the scripture *"but Noah."* Praise God, Noah was using his faith! Noah believed God. We can, too! Noah and God talked. We can talk to God and hear Him talk to us too! Noah listened and obeyed God. We can too! By faith and obedience he overcame. We can too! "Same O" I am going to list some thoughts on what Noah had to overcome.

- Not knowing what rain was
- Not knowing what a boat was
- Not knowing what a flood could do
- Not questioning how to build an ark, just followed God's instructions
- Not questioning how to get the animals in the ark two by two, male and female
- Not arguing about the measurements of the ark
- Not giving up because of the scorn and mockery of the people
- Not giving up because of the heavy work load
- Not arguing about how the door would go shut
- On and on it could go -- but **HE TRUSTED GOD BY FAITH.**

He probably was the first "missionary" to tell his generation about God. By faith he told them what he was doing and why he was doing it as they mocked him. I know "Same O" he was the last person to share with them God's love. He shared his faith but each one of them had to accept God on their own faith. I wonder if Noah wished his ark was really a lot bigger. I am sure he must have "shared his heart out" hoping they would listen to him and believe in his God. Noah did not doubt God. By faith we do not have to doubt God. Noah knew what God said was true. By faith we can believe what God says in truth.

I heard it said that man is a spirit being, very capable of operating on the same level of faith as God. In Mark 9:23 Jesus said, *"If you can believe, all things are possible to him who believes."* We find in Matthew 17:20 Jesus is telling his disciples *"Because of your unbelief (you could not cast out the demon.): for assuredly, I say to you, if you have faith as a mustard seed, you will say to this mountain, move from here to there, and it will move, and nothing will be impossible for you."* Mark 11:23 says, *"For assuredly, I say to you, whoever says to this mountain 'Be removed and be cast into the sea,' and <u>does not doubt in his heart</u>, but believes that those things he says will be done, he will have whatever he says."* Mark 11:24 says, *"Therefore I say to you, whatever things you ask when you pray, believe that you receive them, and you will have them."* Faith is conviction, confidence, trust, belief, reliance, trustworthiness, and persuasion in God and all that He says!!

"Same O." I want to share one more story about how faith works before I close this chapter. Let us look at these scriptures: Matthew 14:22-32 and Mark 6:48.

What I am about to tell you is very touching to me because it helps me understand why God does not just automatically stop storms in somebodies life when they pray demanding: "God stop this <u>crisis</u> storm." He will not drop automatically out of the sky, and fix everything, no manner how demanding. Here is why. Listen carefully!

Jesus and his disciples were about to feed five thousand men. Yes, there were women and children on the hillside, also. The people were instructed to sit on the grass in groups of hundreds and fifties. When Jesus broke, the little Guy's love offering of five loaves of bread and two fishes, he looked up to His Father and blessed the food. The disciples saw as they passed out the food that their baskets only became fuller.

The people all ate and were filled, yet there were still twelve full baskets, one for each disciple. Think about what each disciple had experienced. They had been a part of a miraculous banquet. It was almost dark and the wind and the skies were not looking favorable to men that ride the seas. We can hear Jesus <u>compelling</u> his disciples to get into their boat and go to the other side. I have heard it is a two-hour journey from one side of the Sea of Galilee to the other. We find the disciples are on the lake for a good nine hours and they are only half the way across the lake with the water getting rougher. They had not given up in the midst of the storm, they had not turned around and disobeyed what Jesus had compelled them to do – which was, "go to the other side." Interesting, huh "Same O?"

Now look at what Jesus does. He knows he is responsible for theses travelers and we find him getting very wet out walking on the water in spite of the storm. The scripture says in Mark 6:48 that "*he would have passed them by.*" Wait a minute, "Same O" I thought he was going out to help. Notice this point. The disciples have to make a demand on the power of God. Jesus said *"Be of good cheer! It is I do not be afraid!"* They had to look out of the natural and into the supernatural for help. Jesus did not just automatically still the storm. If he could, or would do that, we all would have perfect lives. That is right isn't it "Same O." God wants us to be dependent on Him and ask for deliverance and help <u>using our faith</u>. When we cry and scream at God to do something that is not using our faith, it is bullying God. We must call out for help, and believe that our Redeemer will do His part. He will never fail us. When we ask, believing in faith, we will receive and our joy will be full. Once the disciples turned their eyes upon Jesus, miracles happened. Jesus stepped into the boat and they were translated to the other side. Now that is a thrill ride not to be forgotten!

APPLICATION

The bread of life, His Word, is the food of faith!
Focus on the spiritual and get out of the natural.
In a crisis we need to expect the supernatural.
We need to walk on top of our problems. Do not default to the natural. Look at the time Jesus raised the son of the Widow of Nain. Jesus said to her, "Do not weep." Why didn't Jesus just raise her boy from the dead so she would stop weeping!!

BECAUSE THERE ALWAYS HAS TO BE A RESPONSE OF FAITH.

God has to have something to flow through. Change happens according to the "power" that works within us. Ephesians 3:20 says, *"Now to Him who is able to do exceedingly abundantly above all that we ask or think, according to the "power" that works in us."*
That power is your faith.
Romans 10:17 *"Faith comes by hearing and hearing by the Word of God."*
Mark 11:24 says, *"...whatever things you ask when you pray believe that you receive them, and you will have them."*
Desire toward God.
Reach out in simple faith. What is the heart of love?
It is a heart of faith.
Faith and love are kin.
We find in Galatians 5:6 *"faith works through love."*
We have a living Christ.
The Lord Jesus is still alive and through faith, those who are filled with His Spirit, continue His ministry.
Remember as a triune being: spirit, soul and body have a specific role to play in our faith walk. "Same O" you have to get all three in agreement before you can move forward.
As we feed on the Word of God, the spirit produces spiritual strength.
That is called faith.

As we develop our faith our spirit will dominant the other two areas and our spirit will be in charge.
The soul must set its mind on "things above."
Mediate on the Word so your thoughts agree with it. Once we get our spirit and soul established on the Word, the body will follow.
The body will do whatever you train it to do.
Teach your body to act on the truth planted in your mind and spirit.
We must bring our spirit, soul and body into harmony – and the Word will take us as far as our hearts will want to go.
"Faith is the open door through which the Lord comes.
Put your whole trust in God and prove Him wholly true.
Faith rests.
Faith laughs at impossibilities.
Faith is the principle of the Word of God.
The Holy Spirit inspired the Word – He is the Spirit of Truth.
As we receive the engrafted Word,
faith springs up in our heart – faith in the sacrifice of Calvary,
faith in the shed blood of Jesus,
faith in the fact that He took our weakness upon Himself.
Faith in the fact He borne our sin, our sicknesses, our pain, and that He is our life today.
Faith is the weapon God gives us to produce our miracles.
God is more than willing to give to all
who reach out the hand of faith."[1]

VII
Love

Because you are born again now you want to please the new Lord of your life. I remember what God said about walking in faith, so my eyes turn to looking at LOVE. Hebrews 11:6 says, *"But without faith it is impossible to please him: for he that cometh to God must believe that he is, and that he is a rewarder of them that diligently seek him."* Then I look at Galatians 5:6b and it reads *"….but faith which worketh by love."* KJV. The only way my faith walk will work is by applying the love of God in my life. First to God, then to me and then to all other relationships. One must learn to love themselves correctly before they can love somebody else properly. If I want to grow out of the "same o's" I must learn to walk in Love using only God's kind of love. The Greek language has at least four words for love, depending upon the situation we are in.

1. <u>Philos</u> is a personal fondness, affection (friendship)
2. <u>Astorgos</u> is similar, but it is more of a familiar love (family)
3. <u>Eros</u> is a romantic, physical love (husband and wife)
4. <u>Agapos</u> is unconditional, sacrificial love (Christ's love)[1]

The Lord Jesus Christ considered this an important enough attitude among His disciples that He actually gave them a command to love one another. He also reminded His disciples that the world will identify with our attitude expressed in agape love. So let us do a check on our love walk.

Please remember now that you are born-again "Same O". You have the Spirit of Jesus in you and all the fruits of the Spirit listed in Gal. 5:22 are in your spirit. But, right now we are focusing on love. For it is by this one, all else works when walking with Jesus. John 15:12-13 says, *"This is my commandment, that you love one another, as I have loved you. Greater love hath no one than this, than to lay down one's life for his friends"*. Agape love is the first and foremost command Jesus gave us, yet all too many Believers neglect to follow it. We expect our "stuff" to change without heeding this commandment. Maybe you have been saved for forty years and have prayed all day every day. But with strife in your heart and not living by the love commandment of Jesus, spiritual things are foolishness to you and you will remain in the "some o's". So let us do a check on our love walk. When we have a particular stubborn problem, we need to put the power of love to work on it! The power of love is the greatest power in the universe. It is beyond defeat, it never fails (1 Corinthians 13:8). The bible says God is love and when we release love into our problem we do release God into it. Jesus becomes responsible for turning the situation around and into success. Are we looking for the power of God to be released in your life "Same O"? Then the love walk is the "switch" to start up the power walk.

God's power package just doesn't work without it. This is one reason why the Body of Christ, the church has failures. We <u>can</u> set our hearts on keeping this commandment, and then we <u>can</u> be confident when using our authority. We can look at our born again spirit and see the "love" fruit-of-the-spirit is in us already. We must, therefore, know we have it and "<u>can act</u>" accordingly if we purpose to walk in love. If this seems foreign to you look at this scripture in Ephesians 1:17 praying *"that the God of our Lord Jesus Christ, the Father of glory, may give to you the spirit of wisdom and revelation, in the knowledge of Him: <u>the eyes of your understanding being enlightened</u>: that you may know what is the hope of His calling, what are the riches of the glory of His inheritance in the saints.* (You are a Saint now that you are born again.) *And what is the exceeding greatness of His <u>power toward us who believe according to the working of His mighty power</u> which He worked in Christ when*

He raised Him from the dead and seated Him at His right hand in the heavenly places." To me that says the power pack is given to me because I am "in Christ". Therefore with His power of love, mixed with faith of God and the Holy Spirit I can do this!! With Him in me and me in Him I can ask the Holy Spirit for help to walk the walk of unconditional love to other people. I can succeed and overcome with the Holy Spirit working in me.

Let us think about some things that love is not. It is not: strife, meanness, anger, resentment, bullying, swearing, dishonesty, selfishness, fighting, and quarrelling. I have heard it said that selfishness is the root of all grief. That sure seems correct to me. Selfishness is nothing other than wanting it all your way. We must learn we are not an island unto ourselves. At that conference table Jesus already had that Covenant of Love in His heart. John 3:16 tells us what happened *"For God so loved the world, that he gave his only begotten Son".* God wanted to give His Love away (Jesus) to the people he created. But again, He lets us make the choice. Why, because He is a true gentleman and a gentleman will never force anything upon you.

I would like to explain what it <u>meant</u> in the days gone by to cut a Covenant. The Hebrew word for Covenant means "to cut" where blood flows. <u>"The Blood Covenant"</u> book explains how the blood covenant began in the Garden of Eden.[2] It had a God given origin. Stanley and Livingstone, martyred missionaries, cut the covenant many times. We have an Old and a New Covenant which the whole redemptive plan swings upon. I am explaining your covenant of Love so stay with me "Same O". There were three reasons for cutting the Covenant with each other: one a weak tribe would cut covenant with a strong tribe for preservation; two, someone else might cut the Covenant to insure neither would take advantage of the other and lastly two men such as David and Johnathan would cut a covenant for their friendships sake. They had different things they did as far as method. One method was an exchange of gifts, then two men cut their arms with the blood dripping into their wine cups, the wine is stirred and shared between the two men. This was perfectly sacred among all primitive peoples. <u>No man broke</u> this covenant. I repeat <u>NO man</u> dared break this covenant. Our society has a hard time accepting this statement. Our society thinks nothing of breaking their word even for such a thing as a covenant of contract. In Livingston's day their word was sacred and these men never broke this "cut covenant". It was perpetual, and indissoluble, a covenant that cannot be annulled. The moment a covenant is solemnized, everything that a blood covenant man owns in the world is at the disposal of this blood brother when in need.

God proved his love to Abram in Genesis 15:8 by cutting a blood covenant with him. Once blood had been shed Abram knew God meant what He said. Abram understood a blood covenant. **Abram knew that once "the cut" was done <u>God would absolutely make good on anything that He promised</u>. It is the same way for us today, on this side of the cross. Jesus blood was "cut" upon the cross for all mankind once and for all and <u>Jesus will make good anything that He promised.</u>**[3] Notice, all that Jesus has is ours because of the "cut covenant", so the least we can do is keep the covenant by giving our all to Him. His love never stopped. The devil thought he could stop it, but you know that is total deception. Remember the devil is the Deceiver. God's love was magnified upon the cross when Jesus died. Let us receive God's love in a real way, first for our personal salvation and then, so we can magnify or spread it wherever our life's journey takes us. We can know God will make good for us anything that He promised us in the Holy Bible. Why is this? It is because God cannot break His Covenant. He cannot forget it nor ignore it. He is the covenant keeping God. As we learn to lean on Him, stand on His word, and trust Him more, the agape love will flow from our life in a greater way, to the point of seeing signs and wonders following us. The compassion Jesus and the apostles of the Bible had for people concerning salvation, healing, and deliverance should be duplicated in our lives today. Only because of a love walk in and for Jesus can this happen. We in God's church really are still writing the book of Acts. Let's fill up on His love like they did and with the power of the Holy Spirit move in the flow of the Spirit with His same compassion. This dispensation of Grace is the dispensation of the Acts of the Holy Spirit. Let us imitate His agape love, Jesus will be glorified and we will be blessed.

APPLICATION

Think about this.
God is in love with you -- so in love with you!
He literally has given you everything He has!
1 John 4:8c says, *"God is Love."*
Remember, you received that when you became born from above.
"Believe the love God has for you.
It has already been released in the blood of Jesus.
Believe the love God has for you.
It has already been released in Jesus' Name.
Believe the love God has for you.
It has already been released in His Word."[4]
<u>Meditate</u> on this scripture I John 4:16 over and over and over.
"And we have known and believed the love that God has for us. God is love and he who abides in love abides in God, and God in him."
Once we release love into every moment, situation, prayer and every thought, it will strengthen you and cast out every fear
that has robbed us of God's greater blessings.
Once we get that <u>into our hearts</u> we will act differently.

VIII

Words

Once we get the LOVE of God in our hearts we will not only act differently but we will talk differently also. We don't just do this one time, it needs to become our life style. Did you know that our words today create our tomorrows! Recall the fact that God created with words. We are created in His image and we can create with our words Oh, you do not believe me. What if you take and innocent child and ream him out enough times telling him with words he is stupid and dumb and will not amount to anything. What do you think you will have in a few years? You will have a child that is confused and hurting emotionally. He is more than likely struggling with studies in school and relationships. I am saying this can happen without even touching the child physically. The harsh evil words created that situation Proverbs 18:21 says, *"Death and life are in the power of the tongue, and those who love it will eat its fruit."* The above is a negative example. What if you take an innocent child and say positive things to him and give him words of encouragement, I guarantee he will excel. Why is that? It is because of the spiritual law of words explained in the Holy Bible. It is just that, God's law! We must read the bible to learn how to walk with God. Just read the following bible verses, meditate on them, and then act them out. Your life walk with God will change for the better. When you make a correction like this the people around you will notice the difference in you without you telling anybody what you are doing.

Proverbs 10:11 *"The Mouth of a righteous man is a well of life: but violence covereth the mouth of the wicked."*
Proverbs 13:2 *"A man shall eat well by the fruit of his mouth: but the soul of the unfaithful (transgressors) feeds on violence."*
Proverbs 12:14 *"A man shall be satisfied with good by the fruit of his mouth: and the recompense of a man's hands shall be rendered to him."*
Proverbs 15:28 *"A man has joy by the answer of his mouth: and a word spoken in due season, how good is it!"* KJV
Proverbs 15:28 *"The heart of the righteous studies how to answer. But the mouth of the wicked pours forth evil."*
Proverbs 25:11 *"A word fitly spoken is like apples of gold in settings of silver."*
Proverbs 26:20 *"Where no wood is, there the fire goeth out: so where there is no talebearer, the strife ceaseth."* KJV
Proverbs 6:16-19 *"These six things the Lord hates, Yes, seven are an abomination to Him: a proud look, <u>a lying tongue</u>, and hands that shed innocent blood, a heart that devises wicked plans (imaginations), feet that are swift in running to evil, <u>a false witness that speaks lies,</u> and one who sows discord among brethren."*
Proverbs 30:5 *"Every word of God is pure: He is a shield to those who put their trust in him."*

Jesus said, in Matthew 4:4 *"....Man shall not live by bread alone, but by every word that proceeded from the mouth of God."* What feeds our born again spirit? It is the Word of God that feeds the spirit man just as bread feeds the body. Food has to be built into our body. It is the same thing with the Word of God. It has an accumulative effect too. God wants us to feed on His Word to grow in strength and in faith and to bear fruit in due season. We must consume the Word of God to be able to speak forth the words God wants us to share. We are to be the Light of the world and must not cause darkness with our mouth.

Believers, we MUST be very conscious of our words and stop strife for it is a danger God warns against. James 3:16 says, *"For where envying and strife is there is confusion and every evil work."* KJV. We must make up our minds that by the power of God I am not going to let anything steal my peace. Then, when I start to get upset about something, I can first submit to God and remember His promises and then I can rebuke that strife in the name of Jesus and resist it. I can say right <u>out loud</u>, "I am walking in the peace of God today." Those words will make the devil turn his tail and run in the opposite direction. See, I told you "Same O" your words are life or death. In this example, death to Satan. That should encourage you. When you chase the devil off it brings life to your situation. Any situation!

This brings me to another topic of prayer and the law of spiritual praying. When we expect <u>God</u> to chase off the devil it will never happen. You know why? It is because in the Garden of Eden God gave all authority to man. We talked about that in Chapter One. Then man FELL and gave all man's authority to the devil. BUT GOD, gave his son who died on the cross, rose again and bought it all back by the blood of the lamb shed on that cross. Jesus told mankind before he left this earth *"All authority (power) is given unto me in heaven and earth."* Me means Jesus. He took it all away from Satan. JESUS COULD SAY it this way *"Go take this power I died for, I'm giving it back to you, now go use it. I bought it back at the price of my life on the cross where my blood was shed not just for the forgiveness of your sin, but also for your deliverance, and the healing of your body, and soul. Receive it and then freely give it away."* *"Go* (He is talking to you and me) *therefore and make disciples of all nations, baptizing them in the name of the Father, and of the Son, and of the Holy Spirit. Teaching them to observe all things that I have commanded you: and lo, I am with you always, even unto the end of the age (world)."* That is quoted from Matthew 28:18-20. He said in Mark 16:15-18, *"Go into all the world, and preach the gospel to every creature. He that believes and is baptized will be saved; but he who does not believe will be condemned (damned). And these signs shall follow those who believe: in My name they will cast out demons; they will speak with new tongues; they will take up serpents; and if they drink anything deadly, it will by no means hurt them; they will lay hands on the sick and they will recover."* Believe it, receive it, and walk in it, do it, and they SHALL recover. Oh, our words are so important we build or break with them. We bind or loose with them. In a chapter

47

on **PRAYER** I will cover this some more. Please notice the use of words in all this and what we are expected to do with our words. We are to do what Jesus did. We must grow up in this spiritual law concerning words.

In a 2013 quarterly magazine entitled **Concepts of Faith** I found some very interesting concepts about the creative power of God and how it all hangs on our great confession. Note "most Christians who are defeated in life are defeated because they believe and confess the wrong things. They have spoken the words of the enemy. These words hold them in bondage. Proverbs 6:2 says, '...*Thou art snared with the words of thy mouth.*' Faith-filled words will put you over. Fear-filled words will defeat you. Words are containers.[1] Believe that "Same O." They carry faith, or fear, and they produce after their kind." This author had the following revelation from Jesus, "I have told my people they can have WHAT THEY SAY, but they are SAYING WHAT THEY HAVE".[2] Think about that one "Same O". Ponder that one reader. Get a hold of it and you will change the way you talk. Reading in the KJV Mark 9:23 *"Jesus said unto him 'If thou canst believe, all things are possible to him that believeth'."* Matthew 17:20 says, "And Jesus said unto them,....*' for verily I say unto you, If ye have faith as a grain of mustard seed, ye shall say unto this mountain, Remove hence to yonder place; and it shall remove; and nothing shall be impossible unto you'.*" Read Mark 11:23, *"For verily I say unto you, That whosoever shall <u>say</u> unto this mountain, Be thou removed, and be thou cast into the sea; and shall not doubt in his heart, but shall believe that those things which he saith shall come to pass; he shall have whatsoever he <u>saith</u>."* "WORDS are the most powerful thing in the universe". God revealed, "My (God's) Word is not void of power. My people are void of speech."[3] We need to start speaking what God has already given us through Christ Jesus if we expect to receive it. Let us start making our words work <u>for</u> us not <u>against</u> us.

"Death and life are in the power of the tongue and those who love it will eat its fruit" Proverbs 18:21. Do you really believe it is? It really is! *"It is honorable for a man to stop striving! Since any fool can start a quarrel"* that is Proverbs 20:3. Do we believe we have that kind of power? Think about it. We can give life to somebody by using words that uplift and encourage, or tear

them apart. Let us not play the role of a fool, let us learn to discipline ourselves and take the leadership role and stop the enemy from dividing our home, family, and churches by listening to and obeying His truths. God says in Proverbs 19:8 *"He who gets wisdom loves his own soul. He who keeps understanding will find good."* KJV Proverbs 18:20 says *"From the produce of his lips he shall be filled"*. Realize that as you ponder a problem or crisis you can enter your land of milk and honey by speaking in faith. Claim your promise from the Words of life found in the Holy Bible for that circumstance! You must not let anything or anyone talk you out of, or pull you away, from the truth of the promise, from the Word of Life. Do not waver! The devil wants you to waver to get you off course so he can steal the victory from you.

You may be questioning how this works. Here is an example. Let's say your son has lost his job. What can God and I do about that when separated by thousands of miles! A Believer can take Psalm 37:23-24 and apply it correctly, then victory becomes a reality. The scripture reads, *"The steps of a good man are ordered by the Lord. And He delights in his way. Though he fall he shall not be utterly cast down. For the Lord upholds him with His Hands."* First, that tells us your Christian son, a born again believer, who is jobless and just got laid off is still in the hands of the Lord. Second, God did not dump him, or fire him. That verse gives us hope. Hope is necessary to carry on. Third, to expect results from the Word of God we must PASS OVER from the natural to the supernatural.

Do you remember reading about the Passover story in Exodus regarding the night the death angel passed through town? There was great victory the night of that Passover as the obedient Israelites saw the death angel pass over them. <u>All</u> the people of disobedience who did not place the blood on their doorpost had death enter their home that night and the result was that they lost their first born, human and animal. We must yield to God's Words. The Israelites that listened were told exactly what to do to avoid disaster that night! Read it again in Exodus chapters 11&12. It is the same for us today, "Same O." God's word tells us exactly what to do, but are we even willing to read it and take heed? We really need to meditate on the verses and speak the verses that guide us to our victory or manifestation that is needed. The "Word" of God tells us how to avoid disaster today. We must read it and receive from it to be victorious.

Let us look at Jesus, our example, whom we are supposed to imitate. The Amplified Bible says in Ephesians 5:1 *"Therefore be imitators of God [copy Him and follow His example], as well-beloved children [imitate their father]."* Do you remember Jesus always looking to His father before he did something? Mark 6:41 reads *"And when he had taken the five loaves and the two fishes, He looked up to heaven, and blessed, and broke the loaves, and gave them to His disciples to set before them; and the two fishes divided them among them all."* He remembered to look out of the natural in which he was (this earth) and into the realm from where the power or provision would catapult - that being God's kingdom! His heavenly home in heaven. He knew his Father was always faithful. Hebrews 10:23 says, *"Let us hold fast the profession (or confession) of our faith without wavering; for he is faithful that promised."* He knew his Father always performed His Word. Romans 4:21 reads *"And being fully persuaded that what He had promised, He was also able to perform."* Jesus is our example of taking a promise and expecting power and provision and protection.

Our words as well as our heart must be established in the Word. James 1:8 says *"A double minded man is unstable in all his ways."* In order to be single minded, we must have our heart established on the TRUTH of the promise. Our mouth speaks what is in our heart. Proverbs 23:7 says, *"....for as he thinketh in his heart, so is he....."* If our words are not in agreement with "the promise", we are not established. We will nullify the answer. Also, our behavior (our actions) must line up with the promise we are speaking in order to receive our needed manifestation. Matthew 12:37 says, *"For by your words you will be justified, and by your words you will be condemned."* So let us always speak words of life over ourselves and others.

What a privilege to speak God's truths. What a privilege to team up with the God of the universe and use our words to honor Him and thus help mankind be what God would honor. James 3:2b-6 says, *"If anyone does not stumble in word, he is a perfect man, and able also to bridle the whole body. ….. Look, at ships, although they are so large and are driven by fierce winds, they are turned by a very small rudder wherever the pilot desires. Even so the tongue is a little member, and boasts great things. See how great a forest a little fire kindles! And the tongue is a fire, a world of iniquity (sin). The tongue is so set among our members that it defiles the whole body, and sets on fire the course of nature; and it is set on fire by hell"*

THIS VERIFIES THE IMPORTANCE OF OUR WORDS.

Let this be our Creed
To laugh when the clouds are darkest,
To smile in the midst of pain,
And remember the golden promise
Of the rainbow after rain.
To say a kindly word
To all who pass along,
To keep content within my heart,
And on our lips God's song. __Unknown

APPLICATION

Psalm 95:1 *"O come, let us sing to the Lord! Let us shout joyfully to the Rock of our salvation."* The next time you are in church and YOU are singing, sing like you mean it! God is listening. Sing out those words unto Him in <u>great praise</u>. We cannot lose doing this, but we sure will gain strength in the eyes of God, for God inhabits your praises. Psalms 22:3 The scripture says in Proverbs 4:20-22 *"....incline your ear to my sayings ... keep them in the midst of your heart....For they are life to those that find them, And health to all their flesh."*
We must watch our words all day long when it comes to politics, health, kids, husbands, and the dog. You are catching on, "Same O".
Matthew 12:37 says, *"For by your words you will be justified, and by your words you will be condemned."*
We either bless or curse with our words. We win all the way around when we obey HIM!
When you pray, pray the WORD of God. Why, because we know from Daniel's prayers in chapter 10 and12 that God said *"thy words were heard, and I am come for thy words."*
God moves when a prayer is prayed accordingly to His Word.
He needs you, (all of us) to be praying His will found in the Holy Bible.
When you pray the Word you are definitely praying God's will.
When you "stand" on the word you bring life into the situation.
When you "speak" the Word you are speaking life.
That is what we want - a LIFE that builds our tomorrow
in a positive way.

IX

Keep Your Heart

"Same O" let us think about the condition of our heart in this chapter and see if we can find a clue to the reason for life being "same o" "same o". In Mark 3 we see the Pharisees had a hardened heart condition that grieved Jesus. Take time to read Mark 3 right now and you will see what I am talking about. God was right there in their midst, his name was Jesus but they could not see him! The Pharisees were the people that knew the Scriptures backward and forward, but they could NOT see Jesus in real life when Jesus was standing right by them literally. Jesus met the messianic prophecy but their hearts were so insensitive they were blinded. Not only that, their hearts were so hard they were insensitive to the needs of the people that lived around them.

    I want to share another time when the Pharisees, scribes and Jews and a crowd of the thousands exhibited hardened hearts. They were celebrating the Jewish Passover. It was a celebration for families and close friends. Jesus desired to spend time with his twelve chosen disciples around the table at sundown. Jesus was instituting His "New Covenant" at the Passover supper. Yet we find tens of thousands of Jews celebrating the Passover this particular year, and for many - the year's observance was <u>indistinct</u> from the last. They had no idea that nearby the LAMB of GOD LIFTED THE CUP OF REDEMPTION and offered it to all. The one who created time submitted Himself to it. He was offering redemption to anybody who would believe in Him. Hardened hearts did not see Him, although He was talking to them face to face. Their hardened hearts could not even see Him; therefore, they would not believe Him. This causes one to lose out on any promise from above. Any promise, yes any promise offered to mankind.

What if the Israelites had not believed the instructions of Moses given by God for the first Passover? The following is a short version of the Passover by Stephen M. Miller. Exodus 12:12 *"I will pass through the land of Egypt and strike down every firstborn son and firstborn male animal in the land of Egypt."* Before the last and most heartbreaking of the ten plagues, God tells Moses to have the Israelites prepare a special meal. It will be their last supper in slavery. It will become a ritual meal that Jews, even 2,000 plus years later will still celebrate every spring. (That is what was happening when JESUS LIFTED UP THE CUP OF REDEMPTION at the Lord's Supper table in Jerusalem.) It is called the PASSOVER. The name comes from the fact that a "divine being" passes over the Israelites but strikes the Egyptian households, killing the oldest son, because they saw no need to put the blood on their doorposts. Each Israelite family butchers a lamb and smears some of its blood on the outside doorposts of their home - a sign for God to pass over this house. Shortly after the Egyptians sons die - that very night- Pharaoh sends for Moses. "Leave us!" He cries. "Go away, all of you!" The Israelites are gone before sunrise. God tells Moses to make sure the Israelites commemorate this day each spring by eating a Passover meal. It's a meal full of symbolism to remind the Israelites what God did for them."[1]

Likewise today we commemorate the Lord's Supper because it too reminds us of what Jesus has done for us. Had the Israelites not put blood on their doorposts, their first-born son and first-born animals would have died. Today if we do not believe in Jesus and what he has done for us, we too will die in our sin. We will never see Heaven, the home of Jesus. We will never experience the love and the promises that are OURS in the Holy Bible. This is so sad because they are already bought and paid for, by the blood of Jesus at Calvary. These promises are meant to help us in our daily walk and bring us victory in the here and now on this planet earth.

Back to the Pharisees and their hardened hearts. Read Mark 3 again and you will notice what they were doing. They were CRITICIZING the Preacher, the minister of God. They were protecting their religious TRADITIONS. They were DISOBEYING the Word of God which we have already established as our absolute anchor. They were WORRYING only about themselves. Have you been on that walk? I think we have all been there to some degree.

The chapter on WORDS, when reread, tells us why it is wrong to criticize. Do you roast the Preacher at your dinner? The Pharisees sure did? Again the Pharisees were very strict with the law but forgot about their heart. In Matthew 15:17-20 says *"Do you not understand that whatever enters the mouth.... goes into the stomach and is eliminated? But those things which proceed out of the mouth come from the heart, and they defile a man. For out of the heart proceed evil thoughts ...these are the things which defile a man: but to eat with unwashed hands does not defile a man."* Remember our tongue either gives life or death. Today, in the dispensation of Grace, it is not of the letter but of the <u>heart.</u> Let us use our words to encourage and not speak defeat with our words.

Traditions are a killer. Why, because they are not legal in the dispensation of Grace. Traditions are man-made ideas on how to get to heaven without the Truth of the scriptures as the basis for the code used. They are man-made to control people. People are controlled because they blindly follow the leader without checking out what was said in the Word. It is so important to read the Holy Bible and do what Romans 12:2 says *"And do not be conformed to this world, but be transformed by the renewing of your mind, that you may prove what is that good and acceptable and perfect will of God."* So we must renew our minds to the scriptures, expecting the Holy Spirit to lead and to guide. Traditions such as: tongues is not for today, women cannot teach men, my behavior is what gets me to heaven, performance is the way up, makeup is of the way down to the devil, healing is not for today, and all people go to heaven because God is love. These are a <u>few</u> examples of ungodly traditions. These beliefs are ungodly lies. You will not find them in the Holy Bible.

The Pharisees and scribes of old had created so many laws that were not from God and it put people into huge bondages as they tried to follow them. Haven't some leaderships done that today? I think twice about being a teacher of the Word. Then "trey" and even then, much more! People make tradition their God in order to stay in their comfort zone or their power zone. However, this leads to a big black hole that steals, kills and destroys. God is Light and sin is Dark. Remember 2 Cor. 11:13-14 *"For such are false apostles, deceitful workers, transforming themselves into the apostles of Christ. And no wonder! For Satan himself transforms himself into an angel of light."* Religion does nothing for anybody. It is a relationship with our Savior and God that counts for eternity. When it is our heart's desire to love Him more and more, then all the rest will come together. Remember Matthew 6:33 KJV says, *"Seek ye first the kingdom of God and his righteousness and all these things shall be added unto you."*

The Pharisees were worrying about themselves. Likewise when we worry, we are off base from trusting God. If we remember to ask the Holy Spirit to help us we will learn to trust Him in the smaller things like: a school test, or when passing the driver's training test to obtain a license to drive. Perhaps it is trusting His Peace for your first airplane ride. Maybe it is trusting Him for that first job placement you have prepared for and were led to apply for. We can grow in our "truster" the more we look to God in situations and ask the Holy Spirit to help. Psalm 25:20 reads, *"O keep my soul, and deliver me: let me not be ashamed; for I put my trust in thee."* KJV

"Same O" "Same O" here is another aspect to think about, and thus locate where your heart is on this. The fact that God provides clean air to breath, water to drink, food to eat etc. may seem mundane to you. Should it be? We in America have a generous supply of all the above and if we care about others and learn to help the less fortunate we are honoring God. No person is without seed to sow. Remember a sower is never without seed to sow! Question to you, "Same O" are you a sower that blesses others? The chapter on Money explains more about the importance of our attitude toward money and where we spend it!

I cannot close this chapter without referring to a Merry Heart. The following verses found in Proverbs 15:13-16 tells it all. *"A merry heart maketh a cheerful countenance: But by sorrow of the heart the spirit is broken. The heart of him who has understanding seeks knowledge. But the mouth of fools feeds on foolishness. All the days of the afflicted are evil, but he who is of a merry heart has a continual feast. Better is little with the fear of the Lord, than great treasure with trouble."* Verse 23 *"A man has joy by the answer of his mouth, and a word spoken in due season, how good is it!"* Verse 28 *"The heart of the righteous studies how to answer..."* Verse 33 *"The fear of the Lord is the instruction of wisdom, and before honor is humility."* Proverbs 23:26 reads *"My son, give me your heart, And let your eyes observe my ways."* This, "Same O", is talking to a person that has placed his faith in God and the "same o" "same o's" are beginning to subside. So this tells us to discipline ourselves to His desires and His ways.

APPLICATION

I learned in Romans 1:21 what causes the heart to harden. I heard a pastor take that verse and turn it around to a positive attitude and this is what I got. Do the following, dear "Same O" and your heart will be softened even where it is hardened in some dark corner.

The verse says they glorified him not as God.
So let us <u>glorify Him as God</u>. Do it in your life!
Next it says they were not thankful.
So let us <u>be thankful</u> in all that is before us.
The verse also says they became vain in imaginations. The Holy Bible says in 2 Corinthians 10:4-5 *"For the weapons of our warfare are not carnal but mighty in God for the pulling down of strongholds, casting down arguments (imaginations), and every high thing that exalts itself against the knowledge of God,*
bringing <u>every thought into captivity</u> to the obedience of Christ."
So let us remember to pull down vain imaginations.
We must remember Paul says we have this spiritual authority.
So DO IT!
The heart can become so dark it is given up to uncleanness of worshipping the creature more than the Creator (Rom. 1:25). So learn to judge yourself and God will not judge you. 1 Corinthians 11:31 says *"For if we would judge ourselves we would not be judged."* John 3:17 reads *"For God did not send His Son into the world to condemn the world, but that the world through Him might be saved."*
Jesus didn't come into the world to execute judgment.
Nevertheless the inevitable result of His coming
is judgment because some refuse to believe.
God will lead you to repentance and lift you higher whenever you reach out to him.
Humble yourself and discipline yourself to do these things.
They are a necessity for a mature walk in Christ. Proverbs 15:33 says,
"For the fear of the Lord is the instruction of wisdom: and

before honor is humility." If you still want to "do" something "Same O", do the following and you will find yourself glorifying Jesus - and that will improve your tomorrows!

"DO"
GLORIFY GOD
BE THANKFUL
PULL DOWN VAIN IMAGINATIONS
WORSHIP ONLY THE CREATOR
JUDGE YOURSELF
HUMBLE YOURSELF
DISCIPLINE YOURSELF
FEAR ONLY YOUR LORD

X
Evolution

Is evolution an innocent thought? Let us look at where we see it being taught. How about National Parks, museums, movies, preschool through high school, colleges, universities and some churches. Today you will find it in many places. Does our Christian philosophy line up with the Bible or do we just take what will fit into our life style so we can stay comfortable? I have heard it said this way. In the Garden of Eden, Satan challenged Eve about the Word of God. Did God really mean what he said? Does what He says really mean anything or is there a better way in life? We need a philosophy that God's Word is accurate to the last detail! I have to believe the Bible does not contradict itself. Contradiction comes when man puts his ideas into the mix instead of letting the HOLY SPIRIT lead and direct. Our philosophy should be that God's plans are better than mine and God is a good God always!!

God created the heaven and earth in six days and rested on the seventh. Genesis 1:1 says, "In the *beginning God created the heaven and the earth."* That is a fact! Evolution is not a fact. It is <u>not</u> an established fact. The Bible doesn't teach evolution and if you believe it you will be rejecting the truth of the Word. Genesis 7:14 tells us *"They* (meaning Noah and his family), *and every beast after his kind, and all the cattle after their kind, and every creeping thing that creeps on the earth after its kind, and every bird after its kind, every bird of every sort."* They were created by God, and they only reproduce after their kind. They may change in their species horizontally but they will never change vertically into another level. Meaning no bird can become a fish. No plant can become a human. Nor can any animal become a man. Our culture today has a motive and desire to explain away the Godly creation. They want to explain it away by happenstance. People willingly and ignorantly choose it. Learn to examine what you listen to and pick up on. You should ask God to show you the Truth by the leading of the Holy Spirit.

Dr. Carl Baugh from Glen Rose, Texas is a man who was once an atheist. He has many degrees behind his name plus many years as director of excavating work. He has done over 2,000 interviews on creation verses evolution. It was his work in the excavating that really opened his eyes to the truth. As an atheist he had taught evolution. But, he saw the facts of science open up to him in the "hands on" and the reality of it all. In the year 1982 at Glen Rose, Texas, Dr. Carl Baugh found a set of human and dinosaur footprints interlocked. This science has proven the Biblical Creation correct. There they found seven human footprints and "dino" footprints intruding each other. These footprints were "tested" and were proven real and indicated that the dinosaurs lived and interacted together with man. Dr. Carl has the "the Wall of Truth" in his museum. It is a geologic column and all genuine. The evolutionists say the bottom layer is 550 million years old. The "Wall" is a correct geological column. According to the evolution theory it shows the proven science of a human sandal in the bottom layer of granite. That blows their theory. Next came the coal layer with a man-made cup found in it. Again it blows away their entire "time table" of millions and millions of years. On or near the top of the "Wall" is a huge dinosaur bone where people are still excavating. Above that is a hammer in a rock that is supposed to be 140 million years old. Next came the human finger in an area under 10 million years old. Among the layers are plants standing that prove the next layer formed rapidly. That area according to evolutionists would have taken millions of years. But in TRUTH, it was all caused extremely fast by the flood of Noah's day. The column doesn't represent what we have been taught about evolution. Evolutionists say it happened in 550million years. Scripture says "Let the dry land appear --" Note also, the base of the "Wall" is granite. Evolutionists say it is 550 million years old. Scripture says - "Let it appear!" It was made not over millions of years but in the time it takes to snap your finger.

Scientifically Dr. Baugh proved to himself that creation as in the Holy Bible was correct-not the evolutions theories he had upheld. Much of his study was done in Israel and in the USA, in the Lone Star state of Texas by the Paluxy River near Glen Rose. Evolution changes things but that change has limitations! It never leads to a higher order. It always evolves downward. But, evolutionists say it evolves into more complexities into a higher order. This is not true. Look at a man. The older he gets the more deterioration takes place. All things spiral downward and decay, versus moving upward into more life of some kind. I have heard it said that evolution has seven assumptions it adheres to. Creation has one calling card, it demands a Creator. One reporter that interviewed Dr. Baugh asked him "What keeps you going, for I know you have had a lot of opposition." The reporter said, "It must be your faith." Dr. Carl Baugh said "No, it was the scientific facts that spoke for themselves." He further added, "The atheist had to have more faith than he did, because he (Dr. Baugh) only needed, and did have, the scientific proof. The facts spoke for themselves."

Dr. Carl Baugh's "Creation Evidence Museum" is in Glen Rose, Texas today. He has studied this for forty years now. The one thing he wanted to know was why the dinosaurs grew so large. So he searched and searched. He knew they could be seventy feet tall and standing up they could be 90 feet tall and weigh 200,000 pounds. There are facts/reports that prove the preflood (We are talking Noah's flood "Same O.") conditions had plants that grew astronomically. There were giants before the flood also. The bible talks of one guy 13 feet tall. (Please look up 1 Samuel 17:4 and 2 Samuel 21:20.)

In the Glen Rose area they proved that humans and dinosaurs lived together. However, the evolutionists believe that the dinosaurs lived 64 million years ago and the first primitive man appeared two and one half million years ago. The point being, the footprints could not be found together. Dr. Carl Baugh, himself, found them together in the limestone rock layer that he and his group were excavating. They were tested by the scans and the density compression tests and they were proven authentic. In late March or early April of 1982 an edition of the STAR paper of Fort Worth, Texas had this headline "TRACKS STEP ON EVOLUTION." Dr. Carl Baugh actually found the proof; that dinosaurs and man lived together at the Paluxy River. Think about that statement: man and dinosaurs lived at the same exact time. Dr. Carl Baugh found the footprints of the two species that interlocked one another in several locations. Dr. Baugh said he could not sleep for four nights because it proved he was wrong in clinging to the theories of evolution. Ernst Mayr; an American who was a professor at Harvard, and was the leading evolutionary biologists of the 20th century, had said in a debate with a creationist, "If it is proven that dinosaurs and man lived together, evolution is destroyed."[1]

APPLICATION

What is the one and only absolute thing that we have today?
The answer is the Holy Bible.
Remember we know you can hang your hat on what God says!
You must renew your mind, Romans 12:2 (there it is again "Same O")
or at least admit you do not know it all?
You must renew your mind, or at least admit you are not always right.
You could and should bow your head and ask the Creator –
"Who is right-the Creationist or the Evolutionist"
Is it: A - Creationism
Or: B - Evolutionism
To make that work you must be able to hear God and know you have heard the voice of God. Then don't argue with Him.
If you are not there forget that!
You could go down to Paluxy River and check into a Hotel/Motel on a Saturday that Dr. Carl Baugh is there and take a tour through the visible facts of science. You could see "the Wall" for yourself, and listen to a "talk" given by Dr. Carl Baugh about all that has been proven in favor of Creationism.
Check it out and book your vacation time as a time of fun looking with an <u>open mind</u> to your Creator.
He made you, you complex thing!
Go and renew your mind and enjoy that vacation.

XI

Body, Soul and Spirit

We mentioned in passing that we are a body, soul, and spirit. We are a three-part being. We are created in His image. God is a three-part being, and we are a three part being. Psalm 139:13-16 (LASB) reads *"For you created my inmost being; you knit me together in my mother's womb. I praise you because I am fearfully and wonderfully made; your works are wonderful, I know that full well. My frame was not hidden from you when I was made in the secret place. When I was woven together in the depths of the earth, your eyes saw my unformed body. All the days ordained for me were written in your book before one of them came to be."* God says in Ephesians 1:4 *"...He has chosen us in him before the foundation of the world, that we should be holy and without blame before Him. In love He predestinated us unto the adoption of children by Jesus Christ to himself."* KJV This is saying that God, who is the Trinity, loves us so much He worked out a special plan for our lives. We too, are a trinity in the sense we are a three-part being made up of a spirit, soul and body. Jeremiah 29:11 reads *"For I know the thoughts that I think toward you, says the Lord, thoughts of peace, and not of evil, to give you a future and a hope."* A life of love, success, happiness, health, and heroics that bring pleasure to God and His kingdom is what God has planned for each person. God's plan for each of us is a plan that supersedes all our thinking. But, we have to choose it. Choose we must. We choose good and/or bad, and accordingly things begin to happen. People take Ephesians 1:4 and think "I am in trouble (of some kind) and this is what God has for me."

WRONG! God does not plan bad stuff for your life as: your marriage falling apart, and kids to dying at a young age etc. We live in a fallen world: we must fight the flesh which includes the mind, (which needs to be renewed) and we also have a demonic force out there to come against us and defeat us. Remember we are winners in Christ. In 1 John 4:4 it says *"You are of God, little children, and have overcome them: because He who is in you is greater than he that is in the world."* We must choose those things that honor God and his kingdom to flourish in the success and joy that is ours in Him. <u>We must get our mind lined up with what God has lined up for us</u>. When those truths drop into our heart they manifest in a victory for us. They have become revelation knowledge.

You see when you are born again you are a new creature! In Second Corinthians 5:17 it reads *"Therefore if anyone is in Christ, he is a new creature; old things are passed away; behold, all things are become new."* This means of the three-part you, your spirit is no longer the "sin nature" you were born with because of the FALL of Adam. The old nature is gone and God puts into you His Spirit, just like He did when Adam was first made <u>before</u> the fall. Now in your spirit you are a brand new species. Praise the Lord!!! Now you can communicate with God just like Adam did before he committed high treason. Adam talked to God and God talked to him. They enjoyed each other. God was blessed and Adam <u>was delighted</u> (Genesis 1 and 2).

Being a brand new species we see our spirit is brand new, totally new. The body and the soul are not! Some Believers say, "I can sin with the best of the unbelievers." Let us look at 1 John 3:9 *"Whoever has been born of God does not sin; for His seed remains in him; and he cannot sin, because he has been born of God."* That verse says your spirit cannot sin. Only your mind and body can. Romans 6:3 says *"Or do you not know as many of us as were baptized into Christ Jesus were baptized into His death?"* Your spirit in you died and it is now the new creature, new species, born-again. Your spirit is just like God's spirit. That spirit that separated you and me from God is changed. I am now born from above. No more old nature. Romans 6:4 says, the *"Old spirit is buried - dead."* Romans 6:6 says, *"…knowing this our old man was crucified with Him, that the body of sin might be done away with, that we should no longer be slaves of sin."* Whether you let the carnal nature dominant your life is dependent on whether you <u>know</u> some things!

Look at Romans 6:6 *"Knowing this, that our old man was crucified with Him..." "Knowing this"* you have to know something to resurrect this life that is in you which can be called "the fullness of God." If born again, God's fullness is in you. What do I have?

I will mention just a few benefits: we have the mind and the faith of God, all the fruits of the Spirit, and His resurrection power in our born again spirit. Yes, they are on the inside of you. Whether a person has this manifested in their life depends on them "KNOWING THIS" - YOU HAVE TO RENEW YOUR MIND. Proverbs 23:7 says *"For as he thinks in his heart, so is he...."* Reader are you catching on, on how to get out of "the same o's". Your life goes in the direction of your thoughts correct or incorrect thoughts - your life will go in that way even when born again. <u>You have to renew your mind to who you are in the Spirit.</u> I am three parts. When your soul (MIND, WILL, EMOTIONS) are renewed you have two parts agreeing (spirit and soul) then the rest (which is the body) will line up shortly.

Think about this "Same O". When the mind is in agreement with the flesh that says 'I am only human' the resurrected life will <u>not</u> manifest. What do I have to know? Romans 6:6 *"our old man is crucified with him (Jesus) that the body of sin might be done away with, that we should no longer be slaves to sin."* Now I know: my old nature is taken out of me and, I have a brand new nature; my nature is changed, that is the part of me that is my spirit. I am no longer a sinner saved by grace. I <u>was</u> a sinner; now at the core I am brand new. That doesn't mean all the resurrection power shows up. NO, as you think you will "do". WE MUST RENEW OUR MINDS! That is the key<u>: to stop identifying with sin as a part of us.</u> Do not **see** yourself an old sinner. **See yourself as a brand new being free from sin**. Born again people have a new core and we must <u>stop </u>identifying with the old self nature. When you see yourself only as a man or woman you will live only as a human being, but if you could **see** yourselves as

God-possessed, as God's ambassador, you would live differently. **SEE** yourself as a new person. That old nature was united to the devil. Your sin nature programmed your mind to begin with. The body agrees with wrong thinking so you need your mind reprogrammed. Values, attitudes are often wrong. They need to be changed to agree with what God says. **SEE** yourself changed!!! Identify with your new nature for this life <u>NOW</u>, not just in heaven. We have got the same power Jesus had when he walked on the face of the earth. Walking in the supernatural here, on planet earth, should be the norm. **SEE** who you are **"in Christ"** now! This will start the days of miracles rolling in our lives. It is happening in the Bride of Christ now. I hear those chariots rolling. Let's all join in on this roll, winning the race in victory! We will win only as we persevere in faith according to the Holy Biblical Truths of God.

APPLICATION

You now know you are a three-part being and God loves all three parts of you.
Know when you are born from above you are sealed by the Holy Ghost.
Ephesians 1:13 reads *"In whom ye also trusted, after that ye heard the word of truth, the gospel of your salvation: in whom also after that ye believed, ye were sealed with that Holy Spirit of promise."*
You are vacuumed packed and no impurities can get into your born again spirit.
You are saved for eternal life - now and forever more.
Know now it is up to you to change something if you want something new to happen in your life.
Start by RENEWING YOUR MIND. Romans 12:2 says *"Be not conformed to this world: but be ye transformed by the renewing of your mind, that ye may prove what is that good, and acceptable, and perfect, will of God."*
Start reading your Bible. Start with big John and watch Jesus walk right out of the pages and into your life.
Find a church that believes in the fullness of the gospel.
2 Timothy 2:15 says, *"One must study to show yourself approved unto God a workman that needeth not to be ashamed, rightly dividing the word of truth".*
Check out what you hear across the pulpit in the Holy Bible.
When it is tradition it is wrong. Reject it!
There are a lot of good things available on TV and internet. However there are a lot of wrong teachings out there too, so beware.
You won't go wrong with awmi.org.
As you study ask the Holy Spirit to lead you to the correct mentor in your area.

XII
Mercy, Law and Grace

This chapter is going to cover a time-line of mercy, law and grace. This is going to help you understand why we are completely pure when we believe in Jesus Christ and are born again. Romans 5:13 says *"For until the law sin was in the world: but sin is not imputed when there is no law."* From the time of Adam and Eve up to the time of Moses' appearance God worked with his people through Mercy. As we look at Adam and Eve and what they did in the Garden of Eden we find them fallen. God saw them as sinners, but God did not rub it in. I heard it put this way: God did not show them the seriousness of their sin because he did not want them sin-conscious. Notice that! God made a way of escape for them. He took an animal (The first blood was shed to cover sin, not wash away sin.) and killed it (blood was spilled) to make a covering for their bodies and their fallen spirit, right there in the garden (Genesis 4:21). This was a great act of mercy. Then in Genesis 4:15 we find the mercy of God protecting Cain, the first murderer in the bible. It reads, *"And the Lord said unto him, 'Therefore whosoever slayeth Cain, vengeance shall be taken on him sevenfold.' And the Lord set a mark upon Cain, lest any finding him should kill him."* This is a great example of mercy. God did not rag on Cain, he provided mercy for him in his time of need. He did not condone what Cain had done. He was making a way for mankind to change but, again man missed it and God provided a way of escape using mercy.

How about Abraham. Do you remember how he saved his own skin two times by sending his wife off to satisfy another? Sarai was told to lie to save Abraham's own skin (he thought). She was taken by an evil King who intended for Sarai to join his harem. God had already told Abraham she was the one with whom they would have "the promised" son (Genesis 17:19). Asking Sarai to lie to save his own skin was a huge deception in Abraham's brain because he was thinking of only himself. He actually was jeopardizing the linage of the birth of Jesus Christ. Did God have a hissy fit?? NO! Here was the perfect opportunity for God if he was going to have a hissy fit. No, actually I thought he should have had one for Sarai's sake, but I am not God. (All people can be thankful for that.) God looked down on the situation and applied his mercy again. Sarai was given back untouched, to Abraham, and he had to pray for the king so all the wombs of the king's harem to be opened again. That tells me Sarai must have been there for a pretty good length of time. More mercy spilled out even to the bad guy (as well as Sarai) and Abe's own sinful way of life.

Here is another thought: you cannot steal from God and get away with it. God always wins out at the end. Hey, "Same O" have any of these thoughts clicked to see where you have missed it? Just repent and forgive and change. This alone will make a "same o, same o" life better. When you honor God your life will always be better. Just repent and ask forgiveness from God and/or anybody you need to forgive. <u>Just do it!</u> Maybe you need to forgive yourself. Do it now. You can do this because you live in the time of grace-which we will get to shortly. Back to Isaac the promised son. He did the same thing as his father by putting his wife in harm's way to save his own neck. Mercy is extended again. Man I am glad I am living in the dispensation of grace so these generational curses can be broken by the blood of Jesus. Look at Jacob the Father of Israel. How many wives does he have? He has four. (Their marriage was to be <u>one</u> Adam and <u>one</u> Eve... get the point.) God extended His Mercy again. God did not impute sin to these people. Mercy was theirs!! Sin was not held against these people. But they were <u>not</u> getting the message! People did not see how awful sin was and God had to show them. Perhaps, because of the lack of punishment people thought God was approving of their sin. People do think that way today, too. They had not been paying attention to the reading of the scrolls. Today people do not pay attention to the reading of the Holy Bible, it just gathers dust. The mercy was looked upon as "I can do anything I want and God doesn't care." They had the mentality of "I am right in my own eyes." The law was about to take away this self-righteousness. As these people did anything they wanted the law had "to become" or there would not have been a VIRGIN from which Jesus could be born. These people all lived in the period of time that is called MERCY.

The next time-line slot of two thousand years is called the LAW. People are much more familiar with it. The Law came into existence after the two-thousand years of Mercy, when Adam committed high treason that caused the FALL. We find that when God gave a commandment it was just that, in the time of LAW. Think about that and your own walk with God. Listen to this story that is in the Holy Bible and think twice or maybe thrice before you poo-poo something God commands you to do. In Numbers 15:32-36 God had given the law about the Sabbath. Do remember this is all under the "OLD COVENANT"! The words were DON'T DO - IF YOU DID - HARSH PUNISHMENT even DEATH sometimes. This was when Moses was leading the Israelites across the desert heading for the land promised to them. It was called "THE PROMISED LAND". Perfect name if you ask me. We find in this story that a guy broke the Sabbath by picking up sticks on that Holy Day. Moses did not know what to do with him. So I tell it this way. Moses put him in a holding pen and got on his face before God asking, "What now God?" God said "kill him". Note this before you think God too harsh. God gave the law to show sin was unacceptable and meant death. Also, the law put 'fear of God' into man. This is where the "sin consciousness" started. It included condemnation, guilt, and wrong kind of fear towards God. It was meant to show you that you could not keep the law - so throw yourself on God for help and stop trusting in yourself. So what could possibly be next? JESUS CAME!!!! Thank God for Jesus!

Today some people still have this "harsh" philosophy about God. God killed my baby when it died as an infant. God had the tornado blow my house away. God will punish me when I do wrong. On and on it goes. These are just hangovers from the "law days". But, let us stop there for a minute and realize we are now in the last two thousand years of time. This dispensation is called GRACE!! John 1:17 reads *"For the law was given by Moses, but grace and truth came by Jesus Christ." KJV* Can <u>you see</u> that we are in the last two thousand years? MUCH of the OLD COVENANT, PHILOSOPHY OR MIND SET CLOUDS OUR MIND as we must change or renew our minds to what Jesus did on the cross. We live on this side of the cross WHICH IS THE DISPENSATION OF GRACE. The old covenant ways are all finished. Jesus hanging upon the cross said "It is finished". I might add there are other points of life that were finished too, but they are not the point of discussion right now. An example would be Jesus finished his goal or life's destiny here on <u>earth</u>. Matthew 5:17 reads *"Think not that I have come to destroy the law, or the prophets: I am not come to destroy, but to fulfill." KJV* Yes, Jesus fulfilled the Old Testament law. Jesus supersedes all. We are not under law any more.

As I have given an example or two about the wrath of God in the two- thousand year time line of the law we need to realize that this is just a tiny report of what went on in those days. God's wrath was real to those people. God's wrath is real today too, but we have Jesus who stood in the gap for us. The *"law of sin and death"* was in operation during the two-thousand years of LAW. Today we can operate by choice out of the *"law of the Spirit of life in Christ Jesus" (Romans 8:2)*. There is that phrase again "in Christ Jesus." Oh how important it is that we know who we are in Him. Look at this verse in Romans 5:9c *"being now justified by his blood,* (Jesus' blood) *we shall be saved from wrath through him."* We do not receive God's wrath in this dispensation of Grace. God does not pass out sickness or disease to people to teach them something. He does not have any disease to pass out. <u>Did you get that?</u> He does not cause a flood to destroy your house because you have done something wrong, just to humble you or correct you. He is not ever mean. He teaches through his word. Romans 5:12&13 says, *"Wherefore, as by one man sin entered into the world, and death by sin; and so death passed upon all men, for that all have sinned: (For until the law sin was in the world: but sin is not imputed* (NO ACCOUNT IS KEPT) *when there is no law"* KJV. WE are not under law, therefore no account is kept against the Believers. Psalm 103:12 reads *"As far as the east is from the west, so far has he removed our transgressions from us."* Our sins were forgiven long before we committed them anyway, all we have to do is believe Jesus died for our sins and rose again, repent and change by renewing our minds. When you ask Him to forgive you, you can receive from Him and believe Him. Believe what God said we have in Christ Jesus. This is where we fall short. This letter of Romans is written to believers.

A believer today (Meaning those who are born again.) lives on <u>this</u> side of the cross where no wrath of God is spilled out on his people. Romans 8:1 reads *"There is therefore now no condemnation to those who are in Christ Jesus* (who live in union), *who do not walk according to the flesh, but according to the Spirit."* So what is the wrath of God we don't get? God imputed all his wrath on Jesus who carried our: sin, sickness, disease, and poverty, so we do not have to carry any of it. We do not have to be sick, but we must learn or renew our minds on how not to be sick or how to receive our healing. For centuries we have not been taught any of this. Hey "Same O" is anything clicking for you? Do you see where there is a huge hole in your correct learning for your life to blossom? But by the grace of God – we are learning, so keep seeking Him. You see in Romans 4:23 says it is imputed to us for righteousness. Romans 5:1-2 says *"Therefore being justified by faith, we have peace with God through our Lord Jesus Christ: through whom also we have access by faith into this grace in which we stand…"*

You will find Deuteronomy 28 full of blessings of obedience and consequences of disobedience. The old covenant is not done away with, it is fulfilled by the purchasing power of Jesus' blood shed upon the cross of Calvary. We live in the dispensation of Grace and there is no law, so sin is not imputed to me. Praise the Lord! Because your old nature is replaced by a brand new nature, death has no more dominion over us as a believer. If you see yourself inferior to the devil and all his actions and behaviors you will only give token resistance to the devil when he comes around with lies, deceptions and other sensual tactics. Yes, you will find yourself sinning right along with the rest of them. Think about this. God only sees you as who you are in your spirit: which is righteous, pure and white as snow as found in Psalm 51:7 *"Purge me with hyssop, and I shall be clean; wash me, and I shall be whiter than snow."* (That old testament man knew he could be washed white as snow as he looked forward to the cross; we are once and for all washed in the blood of Jesus and we are white as snow <u>now</u> as we look back to the cross.). It is about time we the Believers see ourselves that way. When we do, all the old habits and cravings will start to fall away. We need to see ourselves as who we are in the Spirit as in Christ Jesus. We need to go over our list of WHO I AM IN CHRIST and what Jesus has already done for us and start believing and acting like it. We must remember we are <u>not</u> only human! In the spirit we are wall to wall Holy Ghost - that is one third of you. Really! We need to see ourselves as God possessed, because we really are if we have made him Lord and ruler of our life. That is what Grace can do for us today in a short version. It is beautiful and wonderful to see what Jesus really did on the cross. We can be free from hell and go to heaven. We can be free of sickness, and be healthy. We can be free of lack and be prosperous. We are protected at all times by the grace paid for on the cross. This Grace includes: forgiveness of sins, deliverance, healing, joy, and peace literally the fullness of the gospel. Grace is graceful. We need to receive our own personal revelation and walk in it <u>all</u> by receiving in totality His free gift of GRACE.

APPLICATION

Learn to **see** yourself "in Christ" from now on.
Know you are a new creature and Sin cannot have You!
Check out your ungodly beliefs and renew your mind to Truth. This is a biggie. Ask the Holy Spirit to reveal those ungodly beliefs.
Repent and then change as the Holy Spirit leads you into a higher walk with Him.
Look at your "performance-acts", and check your motive for "doing."
If your motive is to get salvation from God by working for it;
you will not get it! Thinking like that is thinking
Old Covenant / Old Testament - you are not living in those days,
you are alive in the days of GRACE.
You did not get to pick the era in which to be born.
You are born into the dispensation of Grace.
Grace is all about God's supply for our needs.
Make Grace the principal thing in your daily walk.
Salvation is obtained solely by receiving His free gift!
The promises are received only by getting out of the law of sin and death thinking (which is sin consciousness)
and into the law of the Spirit of Life in Christ Jesus
(which is Christ consciousness).
When you do something for God, fearing punishment if you do not do it - that is not gospel either, that is a lie figured out by man to control you and put you back into bondage.
So do not receive or follow it.

XIII

The Law

What is the LAW we are talking about? I think most people think of the Ten Commandments first when asked that question. In reality there are many ways to look at this. There is a natural law of gravity. There are laws of geodynamics, and such laws as the rain comes down and then goes back up. I am not going to try to list all the natural laws man has to adhere to or with which they live. As we continue to look at the spiritual side of what God has given us and apply it, we should be able to grow in our application of these spiritual laws and have victories <u>now</u> in this life. That should be a boost - right "Same O."

First, I want you to know the Old Testament law has been fulfilled by the death, burial and resurrection of Jesus Christ the Son of the Living God. Matt. 5:17 reads *"Think not that I am come to destroy the law, or the prophets: I am not come to destroy, but to fulfill."* We do not throw out the sacred ten commandments, we just continue to fulfill them by doing the New Covenant or New Testament great commandment which reads in Mathew 22:37-40 *"Jesus said unto them, 'You shall love the Lord your God with all your heart,, with all your soul, and with all your mind. This is the first and great commandment. And the second is like it: You shall love your neighbor as yourself."* On these two commandments hang all the Law and the Prophets." So we find that the old isn't thrown out but, we are not living under law today! That was Moses' era of 2,000 years behind the cross of Calvary. Remembering we live in the last 2,000 years or era called Grace.

Grace itself has a special place of importance today. It is in this dispensation that the Holy Spirit moves and works through the born - again Believer that is surrendered to God. "Same O" if you want to hear more on that you will have to go to the chapter on Grace. I am now going to list some other spiritual laws, when applied "Same O" you'll find the Prince of Peace alive and working through you. Following God's ways of His kingdom will chase the doldrums of a "same o" "same o" life away.

I wanted to share the Royal Law of Love in James 2:8, the Law of Liberty in James 1:25 & 2:12, and the Law of Faith in Romans 3:27! I am just mentioning them in passing. We have talked some on Love in chapter seven. There is a chapter on Faith Triumphs, and the Law of Liberty fits perfectly into our chapter on Grace!

The Royal Law of Love says in James 2:8 *"If ye fulfill the royal law of love you'll love thy neighbor as thyself..." KJV. "If you really fulfill the royal law according to the Scripture, 'You shall love your neighbor as yourself,' you do well" NKJV.* To interject something about selfishness here. When people are thinking about what <u>they</u> need, desire or must have - love for the people they interact with is null and void. Why? Because selfishness is the root of all grief. If we are just getting for ourselves, whether in action or words, we are not giving to people, and they will not feel loved. If we could look at the people in our lives as God sees them, our reaction to them, and our talk to and about them would totally change. If we would apply love to others as God applies love to us; our world would be totally different. Love each other with genuine affection, and take delight in honoring each other. That is how God wants us to love. His love is pure and holy. Let's ask God to help us love others as he desires. When born again we have his love in us in our new nature, our spirit. Let's stir up that love by praying in tongues for direction on loving our self correctly and loving others through the eyes of Jesus!!! Are you wondering what's tongues "Same O"? There is a chapter on the Holy Ghost which is synonymous with the Holy Spirit in this book that explains the work of the Holy Ghost and tongues. He has many gifts to offer you on your walk with your Lord. Tongues is only one of them.

The Law of Liberty is found in James 1:25 *"But whoso looketh into the perfect law of liberty, and continueth therein, he being NOT a forgetful hearer, but a doer of the work, this man shall be blessed in his deed."* KJV *"But he who looks into the perfect law of liberty and continues in it, and is not a forgetful hearer but a doer of the work, this one will be blessed in what he does."* Remember Grace is free and you CANNOT work your way into heaven. It's a free gift to the ungodly who humble themselves and believe Jesus died that they might have life. Jesus in John 14:6 says *"I am the Way the Truth and the Life, no one comes to the Father except through Me."* So what about these deeds? Paul spent time writing the book of Romans which tells you what Grace is and what it is not. Deeds are done to honor the one whom you love because He's your Redeemer, you're not doing something to get something. In this case deeds will not open the door to heaven. The blood of Jesus applied by receiving TRUTH opens that door to heaven. Truth is Jesus, and <u>He is the only Key</u> to heaven's door. The law of liberty keeps you free of "works". Paul continually tells the people that you cannot mix law and grace or you void your blessings of today. Romans 4:14-16 *"For if those who are of the law are heirs, faith is made void and the promise made of no effect, because the law brings about wrath; for where there is no law there is no transgression. Therefore it is of faith* (and faith alone) *that it might be according to grace, so that the promise might be sure to all the seed, not only to those who are of the law, but also to those who are of the faith of Abraham, who is the father of us all."*

The Jews were constantly pushing the converted Christians to also be circumcised to be righteous. That is a lie and it is law! While Paul and Barnabas were at Antioch of Syria, some men from Judea arrived and began to teach the Believers: *"Unless you are circumcised as required by the Law of Moses, you cannot be saved."* That is Acts 15:1-2 KJV. Paul, Barnabas, Peter and James fell into a fiery debate with the Jews of that day stating that it is by faith and faith alone by which we are saved. Ephesians 2:8-9 reads *"For by grace you have been saved through faith, and that not of yourselves; it is the gift of God not of works, lest anyone should boast."* Works worked in the era of LAW but it does <u>NOT</u> work in the era of GRACE!!! All we have to do is believe in Jesus. Romans 10:9-10 says *"That if you confess with your* mouth the Lord Jesus and believe in your heart that God has raised Him from the dead, you will be saved. For with the heart one believes unto righteousness, and with the mouth confession is made unto salvation."* The law demands but, grace supplies. Remember that "Same O." When born again we must humble ourselves and ask God Almighty where are we tied up in law, in our faith. He will tell us. He will-also help us out of that lie if we ask Him. God is eager for "his church" to walk in the "law of liberty" and then they will be able to receive all the benefits and blessings which Jesus paid for at the cross.

A cross of redemption, liberty, and love is released to man, by putting the Law of Faith to work. The crimson red blood of Jesus was spilled out at Calvary for all mankind but, they must <u>choose</u> Him by using the law of faith. Faith is a live force. Do you believe that? Fear is a force that propels you. You do believe that, don't you? Fear is the opposite and a negative force that tares at you. Faith is a force that gives life to any situation you find yourself in, <u>if</u> you use it. Hebrews 11:1, 6 reads *"Now faith is the substance of things hoped for the evidence of things not seen." "But, without faith it is impossible to please Him, for he who comes to God must believe that He is, and that He is a rewarder of those who diligently seek Him."*

Now let us look at Noah, the guy in the bible with the huge boat. He made the boat under directions given to him by God (Gen. 6:14). It was before anybody had ever seen or heard of anything called rain. Stop and meditate on that for just one full minute, let that sink in. Hebrews 11:7 reads *"By faith Noah, being divinely warned of things not yet seen, moved with godly fear,* (This godly fear does not mean he was afraid of God it means just the opposite. Noah held Him in high esteem and honor. That is why he obeyed Him.) *prepared an ark for the saving of his household, by which he condemned the world and became heir of the righteousness which is according to faith."* Now that is putting the law of faith to work. We are supposed to be doing that too. How? When? Where? Well, let us see in some examples the answers.

<u>How</u> do I write a book when never before in my life I have done such a thing? In faith you say yes in obedience to the call placed in your heart.

Then you ask for wisdom from on High by applying James 1:5 that reads *"If any of you lacks wisdom, let him ask of God, who gives to all liberally and without reproach, and it will be given to him."* You apply the law of faith that God will supply whatever is needed to carry out the assignment. Thus you go ahead and move on the assignment. <u>When</u> do I put the law of faith into action? Whenever there is a need. James 1:6-8 reads *"But let him ask in faith, with no doubting, for he who doubts is like a wave of the sea driven and tossed by the wind. For let not that man suppose that he will receive anything from the Lord, he is a double-minded man, unstable in all his ways."* Did you notice the condition involved?

<u>Where</u> do I put the law into effect? Usually you need to put it into effect in many awkward situations. Don't be afraid to stand up for what is right and use your faith. Let me tell you those words are easy to say, but a whole different ballgame to put into action. Remember 1 Thessalonians 5:24 *"He who calls you is faithful, who also will do it."* Do you remember Sarah's walk in faith with her God? Hebrews 11:11 reads *"By faith Sarah herself also received strength to conceive seed, and she bore a child when she was past the age, because she judged Him faithful who had promised."* Now "Same O" if that is you praying for a child take that verse and stand on it. Do not waver, believe God is faithful to the promise he gave to man in the Garden of Eden, which is to multiply, and you'll have your beautiful baby. That is <u>how</u>, <u>where</u> and <u>when</u> all wrapped up in one excellent example. Praise the Lord! (By the way I am not advocating you should wait to be 100 years old to have your children!) God will honor your faithful stand on His word which is a covenant with you. Be blessed, have two babies, you young complexities. Then remember to lead them to the Lord and teach them to love HIM. Read this "Same O", look at this, it says in Romans 8:27 *"Jesus makes intercession for the saints according to the will of God. And we know that all things work together for good to those who love God, to those who are the called according to His purpose."* KJV Believe that promise for your family!!

I have one more law I wanted to share. It is the Law of my Mind. Romans 7:23 reads *"But I see another law in my members, warring against the law of my mind, and bringing me into captivity to the law of sin which is in my members."* Then verse 24-25 *"O wretched man that I am! Who will deliver me from this body of death? I thank God-through Jesus Christ our Lord! So then, with the mind I myself serve the law of God, but with the flesh the law of sin."* "Same O" are you listening? This takes us back to the understanding that when you are born again 2 Corinthians 5:17 says *"Therefore, if anyone is in Christ, he is a new creation: old things have passed away; behold, all things have become new."* That means your old sin nature is gone and you have a new spirit, a new nature in you unable to sin. It is vacuum packed and sealed by the Holy Ghost. No impurities can get into your born-again spirit. You are like Adam as he was originally created in the Garden of Eden. The flesh is the part of you we can call meat. Before you were born-again there was a sin nature in you. After being born again there is a residual left behind in your flesh that needs to change. If a person smoked the day before they got saved, most still smoke the day after they received salvation. However we must go back to Romans 12:2 and read *"I beseech you therefore, brethren, by the mercies of God that you present your bodies a living sacrifice, holy, acceptable to God, which is your reasonable service. And <u>do not be conformed to this world</u>, but be transformed by the <u>renewing of your mind</u> that you may prove what is that good and acceptable and perfect will of God."*

When you renew your mind to the things of God after recognizing any sin and legalism, things will change for the better and your flesh will line up with the word. My bible says we are not to accept the pattern of an age whose god is the Devil (2 Corinthians 4:4). I like it said this way: Our culture is being genetically altered by the powers of the antichrist. Romans 5:20 -21 says *"Moreover the law entered that the offense might abound. But where sin abounded, grace abounded much more. so that as sin reigned in death, even so grace might reign through righteousness to eternal life through Jesus Christ our Lord."* Grace is right here, if we would just receive the revelation of it so we can apply it in all our life situations. So "Same O" we need not be afraid of anything. Just lean on Jesus, be led by Jesus, and trust Jesus. He protects you (Psalm 91). That is working the Law of the Mind in favor of the position you hold **in Christ Jesus.** When you are

"IN CHRIST" that is your position and you must start rebuilding your tomorrow from a faith based on your standing. This will build a greater tomorrow of happiness and joy. You can do that. God wants you to do that. It is very feasible! It takes discipline but is very possible. With your mind stand on/or apply the scripture Philippians 4:13 *"I can do all things through Christ who strengthens me."* Praise the LORD! That is using faith as a positive life force. That is why you are reading this book, to be able to live a better life <u>now</u> for HIM.

APPLICATION

We live in the era called GRACE.
You cannot mix any law with grace and expect God's blessing.
Our law practiced now in this era is not to be 'hung up' on circumcisions; saying the right number of prayers, baking enough cakes, or attending church enough, tithing enough, and then believing God will punish me if I don't do so and so. God does not punish anybody in this era. All wrath was put on Jesus at the cross.
We are so blessed to be living in the time of grace.
I repeat, God put all the wrath that flew at the people during the era of Law on Jesus at the cross.
All God's wrath was paid for in the death of Jesus.
God wanted the Jews to give him dead sacrifices during the era of Law, the old covenant. These animals were substitutes for worshippers who deserved the death penalty for their sins.
A new covenant dawned.
With the rising of the Son came the era of Grace.
Lifted up on the cross, Jesus became the last dead sacrifice.
His death paid the penalty for all sin.
Today God wants us to be _living_ sacrifices.
We in this dispensation don't have to receive the wrath of God.
Jesus paid for it all.
Look into the chapter of Grace and see more on how we walk in the law ignorantly. These incorrect acts and ungodly beliefs block the blessings of God that are ours.
Again, Jesus paid for them on the cross. If blessings are not flowing to you, a change is needed.
Talk to God about it and listen for an answer.
Then be obedient and act on what you are told.
The blessings will come through obedience.

XIV

Atonement

After the giving of the Mosaic Law, the Law was broken. A priesthood was imperative. With the priesthood was given the Atonement Offering. Prior to this there were only the Peace Offerings or the whole Burnt Offerings. Now God appointed a special sacrifice in which blood was to cover the broken Law, and cover spiritually dead Israel so that God could dwell in their midst. The word "atonement" in the Hebrew means "to cover," and God gave it because of the life that was in the blood. The Covenant Priesthood became the surety of the Covenant. The Priest stood between the people and God. He made the Covering or Atonement for the people. He confessed the sins of the people on the head of the scapegoat, and then sent him out in the wilderness to be destroyed. With the Atonement and the Priesthood, came the Blood Covenant sacrifices. The five great offerings mentioned in the first seven chapters of Leviticus were the Whole Burnt Offering, the Meal Offering, the Peace Offering, the Trespass Offering, and the Sin Offering. These offerings were fellowship offerings and broken fellowship offerings. They had to do with the daily life of the people. When an Israelite was in fellowship, he could bring the Whole Burnt Offering, or the Meal or Peace Offering. When he had sinned against his brother, he could bring the Trespass Offering. When he had sinned against the Holy things of God, he brought the Sin Offering." The above work is bits and pieces of E.W. Kenyon's work entitled "the Blood Covenant"[1]

Hey, "Same O" aren't you glad you did not live in the Old Testament days! Look at all the stuff you would have to line up every time you sinned or displeased God. Think of all the animals you would have to go catch and figure out if it was a perfect, one-year old male, and then somehow haul it off to the temple. Oh yes, "Same O", then there's this manure thing. What do you suppose they had to do with that?? I think that alone would be an incentive to act like an 'angelic being' to avoid any extra trips to the temple! Then the fun began of letting the priest check it out to see if it passed his inspection before the blood flowed. Yes, the blood flowed, "Same O". It had to, to cover the people from their sins. Once a year they had to bring a sacrifice for the yearly forgiveness, but there were many times in between that the people had to bring in an animal to be set free from something or to fellowship with God. That is a lot of blood being spilled. THANK GOD FOR JESUS is all I can say!

Here are some more thoughts from E.W. Kenyon.[2] "The New Covenant has Jesus as the High Priest, and we as the royal and Holy Priesthood (I Peter 2:1-10). In the New Covenant our bodies are the temple of God, and the Spirit dwells within us. Hebrews 7:22 says, '…. *Jesus is the Surety of our better covenant.*' The word 'Atonement' means 'to cover.' It is not a New Testament word, it does not appear in the New Testament Greek. Because the blood of Jesus Christ cleanses, instead of merely covering. The blood of bulls and goats did not cleanse the conscience, <u>did not</u> take away sin consciousness from man. The inference is that there is a sacrifice that takes away the sin consciousness so that man stands uncondemned in God's presence. Romans 8:1 says, *'There is therefore now no condemnation to them that are in Christ Jesus."* The one sacrifice that Jesus made ended the slaughtering of animals, the carrying of blood into the Holy of Holies. It was the end of sin covering. When He had offered one sacrifice for sins forever, He sat down on the right hand of the Majesty on High. This 'ONCE FOR ALL' offering ended the scape goats bearing away sin. Remember the word 'Atonement' means 'to cover.' But under the New Covenant our sins are not covered. They are put away. They are remitted. They are as though they had never been. Hebrews 9:25-26 says.

'Nor yet that he should be offering himself often, as the high priest entereth into the holy place year by year with blood not his own; else must he often have suffered since the foundation of the world; but now once at the end of the ages hath he been manifested to put away sin by the sacrifice of Himself.' The expression 'end of the ages' really means where the two ages met. The cross was where the old method of counting ended, and it was the place where the new time began. The thing that stood between man and God was Adam's transgression. JESUS PUT THAT AWAY. Jesus settled the sin problem, made it possible for God to legally remit all that we have ever done, and give to us Eternal Life, making us New Creations." The scripture that backs this up is 2 Corinthians 5:17-18, *"Wherefore if any man is in Christ, he is a new creature: the old things are passed away; behold, they are become new. But all things are of God, who reconciled us to Himself through Christ, and gave unto us the ministry of reconciliation."*

"Same O", we are so blessed to live in this dispensation of grace. We have it so easy. Let us look to our Savior and praise His name forever. Jesus is our atonement, he took care of it all, and gave us the free gift of salvation. John 3:16 says, *"For God so loved the world that He gave His only begotten Son, that whoever believes in Him should not perish but have everlasting life."* God gave His only begotten Son, but it wasn't only so that people wouldn't go to hell. Jesus saved us from sin, sickness, disease, and poverty. He gave Himself as the perfect atoning sacrifice that He might deliver us from this present evil world. Galatians 1:4 says, *"who gave Himself for our sins, that He might deliver us from this present evil age, according to the will of our God and Father."* That is why on the cross He said "It is Finished." His work was finished. Now we pick up where He left off and march on with the "full salvation message." I humbly bow my heart to my Redeemer, my Healer, my Provider and my KING while taking His message forth.

APPLICATION

Jesus remitted our sins; yesterday, today, and for all our tomorrows.
Talk about a free gift.
He not only cleansed us from sin, but then he gave us salvation.
<u>Salvation is more than just remittance of our sin</u>.
It includes; healing, protection, and prosperity for life on this planet,
<u>and</u> eternal life.
When the church is whole and operating in these gift factors, the
lost will come running to us because they will know we are a peculiar
people and will want what we have!
Abraham had these qualities and we are an heir to him. We are one of
the stars he counted while he waited for his promised child, which they
named Isaac. We are part of the family of God that caused the country
Rahab lived in to melt and become faint at heart because
Israel was alive and marching forward with Almighty God.
Had they bowed their knee to Jehovah, like Rahab did, they would not
have been destroyed. Today we are to represent our God like
Israel did that day and march on, conquering our foes by the promises
given us in the Word by our King Jesus.
Victory is promised to us!
Now we, the church, have to renew our minds and act in accordance
with the power of our Helper, the Holy Spirit, to claim our
VICTORIES.
Let us march forward "Same O"!

XV

Grace

We live in the dispensation of grace. Grace came AFTER the cross of Calvary for all mankind. Grace breaks the dominion of sin. Romans 6:14 states *"For sin shall not have dominion over you: for ye are not under the law, but under grace."* Grace is God's ability given you, unearned and undeserved! Grace is the power to overcome and live a Godly life. Grace is based on what Jesus did, not on what you or I do. If you think you have to perform for God you are under Law. God relates to us based on grace not on our performance. <u>Why don't Christians sin?</u> It is because they have a brand new nature. The old sin nature you were born with is gone! 2 Cor. 5:17 states *"…if any man be in Christ, he is a new creature: old things are passed away; behold, all things are become new."* You can't die to your old nature because it is gone. If you keep thinking you have to die to your old nature, or keep dying to self, you are giving the devil resurrection power. Romans 6:6-11 states *"knowing this, that our old man was crucified with Him, that the body of sin might be done away with, that we should no longer be slaves of sin. For he who has died has been freed from sin. Now if we died with Christ, we believe that we shall also live with Him, knowing that Christ, having been raised from the dead, dies no more. Death no longer has dominion over Him. For the death that He died, He died to sin once for all; but the life that He lives, He lives to God. Likewise you also, reckon yourselves to be dead indeed to sin, but alive to God in Christ Jesus our Lord."* KJV

If you SEE yourself as an 'OLD SINNER' all the time, you are under mining your own ability to change and be who you already are "in

Christ". All born again believers need to SEE themselves possessed by God. Phil. 4:13 states *"I can do all things through Christ who strengthens me."* So it's a lie from hell when you say "I can't stop doing ____" even though you know it is wrong. You aren't SEEING yourself whole! Another reason why Christians don't sin is because it shuts the door on the devil. When you sin, as a Believer, and then something bad happens, it is <u>not</u> God judging you. You have opened the door for Satan to come in and 'eat your lunch' so to say. God isn't judging your sin. I am only referring to born again believers here. God put all his wrath, or should I say all the wrath and judgment we deserved for sin on Jesus at Calvary. We are redeemed from His wrath, we are redeemed from the law. Romans 5:9 states *"Much more then, being now justified by his blood, we shall be saved from wrath through him."* We live in the era of GRACE.

God relates to us spirit-to-spirit now. All mankind is born with the "old man" which is our sinful nature. We acquired that when Adam sinned in the Garden of Eden. Man fell from being a perfect human being to being a man of transgressions. Prior to the fall man had a perfect sinless nature, it literally was identical to God's nature. After all, God breathed life into Him. How could it be anything else? The law was given to man so the "old man" or sinful nature would be recognized as sinful. The law was given 2,000 years after the Fall. The first 2,000 years of man operated under mercy. Romans 5:13 states *"For until the law sin was in the world: but sin is not imputed when there is no law."* The last 2,000 years man lives under grace. Like it or lump it "Same O" it is so. The born-again believer who is saved is dead to the "old man", and dead to the law. Romans 7:4,6 *"Wherefore, my brethren, you also have become dead to the law through the body of Christ, that you may be married to another - to Him who was raised from the dead, that we should bear fruit to God." "But now we have been delivered from the law, having died to what we were held by, so that we should serve in newness of the Spirit and not in the oldness of the letter."* Romans 7:3 explains it well. The only thing that frees us, is being born-again, and then you are "dead to the old man." We must stop, yes stop law mentality and behavior to live a victorious life. That is renewing the mind to who

Building A New Tomorrow God's Way

I am and what I have as a joint-heir to God himself. Again, Romans 6:14 states *"For sin shall not have dominion over me, for I am are not under law but under grace."* What kills Grace in a Believers life is putting oneself under law. You can do it purposely or ignorantly. Are you wondering how that happens? The next examples are thoughts, attitudes and behaviors that put you back into law and therefore the blessings Jesus paid for on the cross cannot be manifested in your life until you change.

When one thinks his church is perfect and it is the only way to heaven that is law thinking. By <u>not</u> reading your bible and finding out TRUTH you cannot compare it to what you hear on Sunday morning, that is the law's way. When you think you have to "do" to get to heaven you are in the law knee-deep. Believing you have to "perform" to keep God happy so_____ will happen, that is law mentality. If you try to manipulate God in your prayers you are under law. Law works wrath and you will always fall short! When you think because I had an argument with my spouse, now God won't love me, or listen to me that's law. When you have an argument with someone just repent to God of your sin and ask forgiveness from the person. Then move on with the peace God gives you because of your obedience. God forgave you a long time ago anyway, at the time he died on the cross. Thinking if I do not tithe God won't listen to me, law, law. If I think I have to dress a certain way or have a certain hair style in order for God to accept me that is law. Maybe that one is easier to recognize. The LAW shows you are guilty and under condemnation. Note this thought from Joseph Prince "The law is called the "ministry of condemnation" because it wasn't designed to make you do right, but to condemn you. And the more you come under the law and attempt to be justified by it, the more you will fail and be condemned by it." "Same O" we can come boldly to His throne of grace knowing that He will never condemn us because we are **in Jesus Christ!"**

Hebrews 8:12 states *"…..and their sins and their iniquities will I remember no more."* How about this way of thinking that, "I have to ____ or God won't bless me," that is law. When you think God sends you problems to 'trib' over and make you a better person that is definitely LAW. You are in law mentality when you think God is keeping score of your daily sins. By believing God is merciful to the sinner, and then hard on that person once saved, law. Think about that one. By thinking that my performance makes God love me more and more, law. When you think you have both a born again nature and a sinful nature you are in law. As a Christian I've a brand new spirit. I have a righteous spirit in Christ and I am no longer a sinner at the core. When a Believer is under the deception that they have to do everything right to please God you are under the Law and not under Grace. The promises and benefits Jesus purchased at Calvary will not be yours. You can change. Your abundant life is greatly jeopardized until you change your way of thinking. Romans 4:14 states *"For if they which are of the law be heirs, faith is made void, and the promise made of none effect."* Think about that "Same O." Does that explain why so many Christians have so many problems they cannot seem to overcome.

Your goodness cannot change your badness nor your badness change your goodness. I'll repeat it again. Your goodness cannot change your badness nor your badness change your goodness. Your core can only be changed by accepting by faith your Saviors blood as your redeeming factor. Your badness (sin) cannot change your born-again spirit that is pure. Your new nature is pure, the old is gone. I believe your new nature is vacuum packed. No impurities can penetrate the seal of the Holy Spirit. Your badness can affect your soul (mind, emotions and will) and body. Born-again believer <u>stop</u> seeing yourself a sinner at the core! For those of you still guessing if you're going to heaven read Romans 10:13 *"For whoever calls on the name of the Lord shall be saved."* Titus 2:1 *"For the grace of God that bringeth salvation hath appeared to all men."* As you read farther "Same O" you will learn how legalism and tradition kill your walk with God. When we walk in legalism and tradition we are not operating out of the law of liberty that has been purchased for the Born-Again Believer. There are many ungodly beliefs that send us down the road into law and thus bondage. Read Romans 5:1-2 *"Therefore, having been justified by faith, we have peace with God through our Lord Jesus Christ. Through whom also we have access by faith into this grace in which we stand, and rejoice in hope of the glory of God."* In Romans 6:19c we read *"yield your members servants to righteousness unto holiness."*

Here is another small list that might have what is needed for somebody to be set free of bondage into liberty.

- God does not want me well - a lie.
- God has no plan for me to be well. Many scriptures tell us *"Beloved I pray above all things that you may prosper in all things and be in health, just as your soul prospers."* Please look up 1 Peter 2:24, and Psalm 103:1-5. It shows that the atonement includes your forgiveness of sin, your healing, your prosperity and much, much more.
- Long hair, jewelry, makeup and movies will send you to hell.
- Thinking you have to do and do and do (performance of any kind), to get to heaven, law.
- Believing healing, deliverance, and prosperity are not for today.
- If you do not read your bible 'so much' you won't get to be with Jesus in heaven.
- Thinking I must tithe or be punished. Actually you end up stopping blessings so you are punishing yourself. God is not punishing you.
- People believe that God will save the awful sinner but puts troubles on the saved one.
- Believing that suffering causes you to be a better person. This is a lie. However you end up using your faith and become stronger.
- Believing that Jesus died for the "godly" and that is why I have to cleanup to receive or reach him. Romans 5:6 states *"For when we were still without strength, in due time Christ died for the ungodly."* So if you think you "gotta clean up" first you'll miss him.
- If you're proud to be "such a righteous guy," you will miss Him. <u>Jesus died for the ungodly.</u> Just a four more.
- People argue baptism of the Holy Spirit is identical to your initial born-again experience and that is a lie. Satan desires people to believe that because then the Believer has minimum authority and power to perform miracles, signs and wonders.

- Prophets aren't for today - not true.
- Healing isn't for today - not true.
- Today there's no need for the fivefold ministry - lie. Those lies keep the church divided and it's no wonder we have so many denominations. God desires his church to be reconciled into one body with Christ as the Head walking in love for one another. Come unto him all you that labor. Remember you live holy as <u>the fruit</u> of salvation <u>not the root</u> of salvation!

I have one more thought to share with you "Same O". <u>Why do Christians sin</u>? It is because they have NOT renewed their minds as to "Who they are in Christ." Religion which is an enemy to the cross messes up the minds of the believer. What God requires of you is to love Him, love His Son, and love the Holy Spirit. They are our God! They want to help us in our daily walk. After a person is born again and has a new nature, a new spirit within, He must learn how to get his body of sin under control by the Word and the help of the Holy Spirit. Read the Word consistently and call on His name regularly throughout the day. If sin is having dominion over you, you're under LAW and not under Grace. A Christian can be saved and still operate under law by his words (wrong beliefs), and his actions (behaviors). That is the body and soul that needs correction. A person under law will run away from God when he fails instead of running boldly to Him knowing he is justified by the blood of Jesus <u>not</u> by his behavior! To change your life you may check out the following. This is a positive way to get out of the "same o's." Do I have any ungodly beliefs? I need to know them for they put me under law. Do I have any ungodly behaviors? It is "knowing" something that will make your life change for the better. If you want a change, doing the "same o" "same o" and expecting change is stupid. Romans 6:6-7 states *"Knowing this, that our old man is crucified with him, that the body of sin might be destroyed, that henceforth we should not serve sin. For he that is dead is freed from sin."* Romans 12:2 states *"... be not conformed to this world..."* God would not command us to do something that we cannot do.

APPLICATION

E.W. Kenyon tells us to remember the Old Covenant was sealed with circumcision, the New Covenant is sealed with the New Birth.
The Old Covenant had the Levitical Priest.
We are now in the New Covenant and we have Jesus as the High Priest, and we as the royal and Holy Priesthood. I Peter 2:1-10.
The resources of Heaven are back of Jesus and back of that Covenant.[1]
When we are born-again we have that covenant with Jesus so He in us flows out of us to perform the things he did while on earth.
This will not happen when we walk in the law and condemnation.
Because of our unrenewed minds and Satanic persecution, we sometimes sin which can cause our fellowship with the Father to be broken, only on our part. Every child of God who breaks fellowship with the Father is under condemnation.
We have an advocate to plead our case before the Father
His name is Jesus.
If we sin and fall under the law and break our fellowship we can run to the throne boldly and renew that fellowship.
We do that by confessing our sin (the thing we just did that was sin - we do not have to get born again again), he forgives us and we are renewed immediately. We do not have to wallow in it, it is over.
We have our joy back.
Note this: we must learn where we fall short and are under law and/or working under condemnation.
Staying in the word, humbly bowing your knee in prayer, and asking the Lord where I have missed it, and listening to his answer
will turn the key in the locked door.
Doing this is the step that will open the door to that law of liberty of Grace and Peace.
"Same O" that is building a great tomorrow.

XVI

Our Covenant

We have talked in a previous chapter about our covenant. Our covenant includes salvation of eternal life in heaven with the trinity, with redemption from our sin as well as protection, healing, and prosperity in the here and now. The New Testament is Our Covenant for this dispensation of Grace in which we now live. Once you are born again, "Same O", I want you to see what you have through the eyes and heart of E.W. Kenyon for he says it so well, "God's righteousness has been imparted to you. That gives you a standing in the presence of the Father identical with the standing of Jesus. If you actually believe the Bible, and believe that God is your Righteousness, and that you are a New Creation, created in Christ Jesus, you will have no sense of sin. That is not as an 'experience' but as a legal fact. This is the most tremendous truth that God has given us in the Pauline Revelation, and this is the very HEART of our New Covenant, that God makes us like Himself. If God declares that you are righteous, what business have you to condemn yourself? When you learn to walk as Jesus walked, without any consciousness of inferiority to God or Satan, you will have faith that will absolutely stagger the world!" "Yet another blessing of your New Covenant is your union with God. When Abraham and God cut the covenant, they became one." "Same O", are you a partner of Christ? Do you dwell in Christ? Does Christ dwell in you? "The incarnation was God becoming one with us. Christ left Glory and came here to be one with us. You and I can stand fearlessly in the presence of hell, in the presence of the devil, as you would in the presence of some little inferior thing. Jesus conquered the devil and stripped him of his authority. Jesus left him paralyzed? You are not a weakling. You stand like the Son of God. You are a son of God. Now we have to overcome the effect of these false teachings." This is why I included "Who I Am in Christ Jesus" in chapter five. We must meditate on it until it is deep within our hearts.

All this fits together to create that abundant life the Holy Bible talks about. Gods' covenant with man includes the "unconditional" gift of salvation or eternal life in heaven with Jesus, which is inclusive of forgiveness of our sin, healing or health as well the ability to prosper. . . Most people see the forgiveness of sin and nothing more. Yes, we are redeemed from our sin but, the manifestation of the protection, healing and prosperity in the here and now comes along with it as we line up with the Word of God - they are conditional. Conditional to what? Conditional to obedience to the Word of God found in the Holy Bible. We are to be a people set apart from the world and unto our God. Our health, prosperity and success will shine as a beacon to a lost world if we maintain our covenant relationship with God. That is because these blessings fall under the "conditional" behavior and beliefs of the Born-again Believer. Salvation is not just for when we die and need to go into eternity to escape hell and go to heaven. I repeat, it is for the days we have to live here, right now. The plan of redemption includes the ability to be an overcomer during the time we live on this earth. How do we overcome people and situations that fly in our face? We must renew our minds to the TRUTHS of the Gospel. 1 John 5:4 says, *"For whatever is born of God overcomes the world. And this is the victory that has overcome the world - our faith."* When we mix our faith with the Word of God, the revelation of the Holy Spirit becomes our bridge to victory and we can continue to march on in triumph. I have heard it asked, "What's the good fight of faith?" The correct answer is "one we win." God has given us the tools to stand up and win. That is what we are going to talk about "Same O". You know by now that one must be born-again to apply these biblical tools that I will now list. Yes, applying them is the key!

TOOLS THAT BRING JESUS GLORY

<u>KNOW HIM</u>
<u>Love Him.</u>
<u>Fellowship</u> with Him.
<u>Praise</u> Him constantly.
<u>Worship</u> Him.
<u>Develop</u> a relationship with God.
<u>Ask</u> the Holy Spirit for help.
<u>Believe</u> the scriptures.
<u>Meditate</u> on the Holy Scriptures.
<u>Put on</u> the whole amour of God.
<u>Faith</u> works through <u>Love.</u>
<u>Pray</u> in your known language.
<u>Receive</u> the Baptism of the Holy Spirit.
<u>Pray</u> in tongues.
<u>Obey</u> the Word.
<u>Go</u> to a Spirit filled church, and fellowship.
<u>Love</u> others.
<u>Tithe</u>
<u>Give</u> of your offerings and time.
<u>Repent</u> when needed.
<u>Receive</u> forgiveness when repentance is asked.
<u>Submit</u> to God first.
<u>Resist</u> the devil second, when needed.
<u>Pull down</u> strongholds and take them captive.
<u>Obliterate</u> all tradition, religious ideas and ungodly beliefs
<u>See</u> the positive blessings and favor of God that are yours.
<u>Boldness</u> to stand when opposition arises
<u>Speak</u> words of God only.
<u>Stand</u> with persistence on the promises for victory.
<u>Trust</u> God and His pure Word.
<u>Sing,</u> dance and laugh your way to victory.

These tools direct us through our life's journey _if_ we use them. Next I would like to tell you "Same O" some of the blessings of the Old Covenant. Now remember Jehovah was the Surety of the Old Covenant in the Old Testament. Jesus is the Surety of the New and Better Covenant. To quote in part only E.W. Kenyon's words from his book "The Blood Covenant" we find the following.

"BLESSINGS OF THE OLD COVENANT"

"God was under obligation to shield them (the Israelites) from the armies of the nations that surrounded them. God was under obligation to see that their (the Israelites) land brought forth large crops. God was under obligation by the covenant to see that their (the Israelites) herds and flocks multiplied. They became the head of the nations and of wealth. There was no city like it no nation like it. They were God's peculiar people. They were the treasure of the heart of God."[1] To repeat a couple other thoughts from his book. "As the Old Covenant was sealed with circumcision, the New Covenant is sealed with the New Birth." "Jehovah was the Surety of the Old Covenant. Hebrews 7:22, '_By so much also hath Jesus become the Surety of a better covenant._' The First Covenant was sealed by the blood of Abraham, (Abe was circumcised – "cut") and God sacrificed an animal (Abe prepared the animals). This New Covenant is sealed with the blood of Jesus Christ, God's own Son." Jesus was "cut" for us and stands back of every sentence in the New Covenant (New Testament)." Just as God stood behind His covenant with the Israelites of the Old Covenant (Old Testament) and was its surety, so Jesus is the Surety of every Word in the New Teastament.[2] Yes, we can build a strong faith upon a foundation like this. If we personally have a covenant with Jesus. "The resources of Heaven are back of Jesus and back of that New Covenant." "What God as Jehovah did in Abraham's and David's days He through Jesus will continue to do for us the same and more." Following this thought line "Jesus is the Lord of all. He has conquered Satan, sin and disease. He has conquered death. He possesses all authority in Heaven and in earth, Matthew 28:18. Jesus then gave it back to us and we are to "Go" Therefore *"We (a Born-again Believer) can act fearlessly upon His Word, because He stands back of it…. He is the Surety of it. He is the Surety of this New Covenant."* I repeated that because it is so important to understand. God please help us all receive a revelation knowledge that all of heaven's ability and heaven's glory and heaven's strength are at our (the born-again believers) disposal. This is the Surety we have in Jesus Christ!

APPLICATION

Pray these prayers for yourself.
"I pray that the God of my Lord Jesus Christ, the Father of glory may give to me the spirit of wisdom and revelation in the knowledge of Him. And that the eyes of my understanding is being enlightened; that I may know what is the hope of His calling, what are the riches of the glory of His inheritance in me a Saint."
Ephesians 1:17-18.
That is talking about all the ability, glory, and strength that is mine and I must receive it and use it.
"I pray that I may be filled with the knowledge of His will in all wisdom and spiritual understanding: that I may walk worthy of the Lord, fully pleasing Him, being fruitful in every good work and increasing in the knowledge God: strengthened with all might, according to His glorious power for all patience and longsuffering with joy; giving thanks to the Father who has qualified me to be partakers of the inheritance of the saints in the light."
Colossians 1:9-12.
A covenant of Grace is a relationship of favor that gives you access to someone else's power.
Now apply that to your relationship with your Savior.
Receive this revelation knowledge from above.
"Same O" that is my prayer, make it yours too.

XVII

Prayer

Think about this "Same O," if the way you are praying is not getting good results, then consider a change in this area. Hopefully this chapter will root out where some changes are needed and you will be able to exchange the old way for a better way and you will begin to see some results. There really are some right and wrong ways to pray. The prayers that offend God open the door to the devil to cause damage. So "Same O" listen up to this partial list.

Some attitudes, thoughts and prayers that offend God.

- Do not pray with a hypocritical attitude! Matthew 6:5
- If you believe the devil can only do what the Lord allows, that means God is using Satan to work good in your lives. Pew! Example: If you think God uses Satan to bring the best out in you through and tribulation that is wrong thinking. God uses the Word to teach you. If you don't use the Word you will learn things the hard way. The hard way is when you open the door to Satan, the world and your flesh. God doesn't use Satan. God doesn't allow Satan to do anything. God has defeated him. We allow him space in our life. We can use our God given authority and stop him.
- Prayer should not be a religious callisthenic to soothe your conscience.

- Praying to manipulate and motivate God to do something is impossible. It doesn't work.
- A wrong motive at heart kills many a prayer.
- Prayer not backed by love profits nothing.
- Fasting and praying to storm heaven for any reason-is really wrong. Colossians 2:6 says, *"As you therefore have received Christ Jesus the Lord, so walk in him."* Remember we never fast to move God. We never fast to get God to do something. Fasting takes us out of the flesh and moves us closer in the Spirit.
- Thinking God is not willing to give unto you – wrong!
- Thinking Jesus love is for "first come only, he gets" – wrong!
- Thinking Jesus's "Love" does end or runs out – wrong!

Christ has already made full provision for the abundant life through His atonement. It is now not up to Him "to do" anything more, but for you "Same O" to receive what He has done. Remember the gospel is good news of what Jesus has done, not on what He is going to do.

- You cannot pray in public - wrong. Just don't pray in King James with a different tone of voice.
- You have to pray an hour a day. That is legalism. If you are stuck maybe the Holy Spirit is saying time to quit.
- Are your prayers repetitive? Matthew 6:7 says, "Use not vain repetitions!"
- Petition prayers should not dominant your prayer life.
- Stop begging for mercy and cleansing! Thank Him for it. He's already done it.
- Stop focusing on your unworthiness, thank Him for His goodness.
- Religion has taught us to expect God to be half way angry with us. True but wrong
- Beware of magnifying the wrong thing in prayer. The thing you magnify grows stronger, the other weaker.

- The Lord can't be badgered into doing something by begging over and over again. Notice God has supplied the need before we have the need. He is not going to run out and do something to draw up your provision somewhere.
- Intercessors today pray for mercy thinking God is judging them. We must believe and trust Christ for what He has already done!
- Begging, pleading, storming the heavens, badgering Him until he pours out His Spirit are all wrong attitudes.
- If you are expecting lightning bolts, or kneeling, or hands held high to be a necessary form to be in communion with God, you are wrong.
- You do not have to impress God, just spend time quiet in His presence!
- Jesus paid for our sin and satisfied God's wrath. STOP begging and pleading for mercy.
- Why do you think God would refuse or hesitate to meet your need? It is because you think God is against you –and that He is ticked off at your ungodliness. That is a wrong attitude. Jesus has it all covered.
- Our inability to believe and receive makes God look like the unjust judge. He is not.
- Jesus did not have "prayer warriors" or "intercessors". He taught them TRUTH.
- Demons controlling cities are there because they derive their power from the people who believe and act out the devil's lies! They cannot be chased out of the sky but they can be chased out of people by sharing the Good News Gospel,

God is not mad at you if you have prayed some of these prayers, but these prayers go unanswered, so please continue to keep an open heart "Same O" to the Holy Spirit as your Teacher and Guide. Do not hold on to unproductive prayer habits.

Some things to remember as you pray.

To pray correctly you need to read, meditate and study the Scriptures.

- On this side of the cross we are to always pray "in Jesus name." He is the author of supply.
- Start your prayer by thanking, praising and blessing Him.
- God has said I am available to you all the time, "I'll never leave you nor forsake you." You can spend all day in communion with God as you do your daily duties. We are to walk and talk with Jesus all day, every day – right!
- In the New Testament days, self-edification is an important purpose of prayer. 1 Corinthians 14:4 says, *"He who speaks in a tongue edifies himself but he who prophesies edifies the church."* Jude 20 and 21 says, *"But you, beloved, building yourselves up on your must holy faith, praying in the Holy Spirit." "Keep yourselves in the love of God, looking for the mercy of our Lord Jesus Christ unto eternal life."*
- Come into God's presence and hear Him say "I Love You"! God is not mad at you, He is always glad to hear from you. When you meet your Savior you will not be judged or condemned, you will be presented your eternal reward. The correct attitude is to enter His court with praise and be willing to be corrected – right on!
- Prayer means "worship," also "to kiss the face". Prayer is kissing our Father's face! Prayer is loving and communing with God.
- Proverbs 18:21 says, *"Death and life are in the power of the tongue, your words produce either death or life."* Praying God's solution from His Word releases life! Praying the problem energizes and strengthens the problem! Did you get that, "Same O"? When our prayers turn to griping, and murmuring and complaining, they release death into our lives through negativity in our prayers. Let's clear out what prayer is not.
- Death and Life are at your mercy!
- God loves faith! He wants you to respond to Him by faith.

- If the Lord has not already supplied your need by grace, your faith cannot make Him do it.
- The Lord needs our cooperation to see His power made manifest or there would be zero sickness on earth today.
- We cannot pray like Abraham because we are on this side of the cross. Jesus has atoned for us. God's anger toward sin has been appeased.
- Our New Covenant has Jesus as our only mediator, intercessor, advocate and surety. He stands between God and man today. Sin is no longer a problem with God like in the Old Testament, because it's been atoned for. God's not angry!
- In Moses' day God's wrath was not appeased and sin had to be judged. Today Christ has borne the judgment for all sin. We can't add to what Jesus has done. They were mediators. We cannot mediate. Jesus is our Mediator. You are against Christ when you pray like Abraham and Moses.
- Jesus + anything = nothing. Jesus + nothing = everything.
- Remember, God is not angry at people anymore because His justice was satisfied through the Lamb's perfect sacrifice.
- If you do not receive Jesus the wrath and judgment remain, and then hell is waiting.
- Hell was prepared for the devil and his angels, not for man.
- Those who refuse to accept salvation by grace through faith are identifying themselves with the devil and will partake of Satan's judgment.
- We don't beg for healing. God has already provided everything you need including healing. He loves you and wants you to have it (Luke 11:9-10).
- God loves people infinitely more than we do, "Same O", but with His compassion in our hearts we are motivated to start releasing the power of God by going out and doing something about it. The Holy Spirit doesn't move independent of people.

- God has already released His power in the born-again believer. We must believe it and start releasing His power to others. For signs to follow we must first believe, go, and do! Consider the fruit!
- You cannot get another person saved on your faith, (Acts 16:31). The seed must be planted, which is the Word of God, for people to receive Jesus.
- Root out wrong attitudes and approaches in prayer, and good results will follow. You can dismantle the roadblocks to hell by praising God, and by binding blindness in your prayers to bring people into a place where they can choose LIFE in CHRIST.

Some example prayers to ponder.

- "I know You can heal me, but You haven't done it yet. How can I make you heal me?" That is unbelief. The premise of that prayer cancels any healing!
- I must pray for the sick today." That is wrong! We aren't to pray for, we are told to heal them. Matthew 10:8 says, *"Heal the sick, cleanse the leper, and raise the dead, cast out devils."* Note the difference of healing them, over praying for them! Jesus completed everything necessary to save and heal every person. We are to be the vessel to believe and receive healing so that we can go and help others receive their miracle.
- People tend to try to manipulate and control God in prayer. "Same O" take a look at your prayers and see what you are doing. Prayer is receiving by faith what He has already done.
- A short prayer can work, *"Peace be still."* is found in Mark 4:39. "HELP" is a prayer! It to works.
- Notice that Adam and Eve never conversed with God over sin, lack, need, problems, repenting, begging, or pleading – yet they talked to God every day!

- You can spend all day with God in communion during all your day's activities. That is prayer!
- <u>Stop praying the problem!!</u> Start praying the desired results using scriptures. Praying God's solution or answer from the Word releases life. Praying negatively and focusing on the problem only energizes and strengthens the problem. I heard it said we pray four minutes in faith and forty minutes of unbelief rehearsing the problem.
- Prayer is not: "Oh God, the doctor said….." Remember we said rehearsing the problem makes the problem energized and the Truth weakens. We are to focus on what the <u>bible says is</u> <u>truth.</u>
- Prayer is not: "Oh God, my husband beats me, and abuses the kids and kicks the cat." This kind of prayer energizes the problem also! Start your prayer thanking Him for something first, and focus on His love, and problems will minimize themselves.
- "Father, thank You, I receive my healing. You never deny me anything good."
- Start your prayers and end your prayers with praise! Then slip in your petition in the middle.
- When the doctor gives you a bad report, don't build it up by telling God Aunt Bessie died of that! That builds discouragement, fear and depression. Pray something like this. "Father, thank You that your name is above every name. Cancer is a name, all alignments have a name. You are above them all! Thank you that You are greater, stronger and more powerful than all of these! Praise Him for His greatness. This is small compared to what you are able to do. So since Jesus has already provided my healing, I will just receive it!" Praise Him some more. This is a winning prayer. Whatever you focus on will magnify in your eyes! God is your solution so focus on Him and your vision of Him will increase! If you magnify disease it will grow stronger. Choose to magnify God not your problem. The one you magnify always grows stronger the other weakens.

Building A New Tomorrow God's Way

- Learn how to fellowship with God in the midst of everyday life. Appreciate him in small things like the flower you'd not seen before and tell Him, "You did a great job!"
- When you pray, "Lord pour out your Spirit for revival," which implies that God is responsible for the dead condition in the church this is a wrong prayer. The church needs to turn from self-destructive ways. 2 Chronicles 7:14 says, *"If my people who are called by My name WILL HUMBLE THEMSELVES, AND PRAY AND SEEK MY FACE, and turn from their wicked ways, then I will hear from heaven, and will forgive their sin and heal their land."*
- When praying for the soul of a lost person you may have to ask several times because a lost person can void your prayers. So pray it until you see positive results. It is not that way when praying for healing for yourself. Here you ask once otherwise you go into unbelief.
- We can pray for laborers to cross the paths of the lost and also bring back into their mind any scriptures they have heard. We can pray His power and protection into their life until they respond favorably.

Even Jesus, the perfect intercessor, could not convince people or set them free through His faith alone, (Matthew 23:37).

Following are some thoughts on what prayer is.

Prayer is conversation with God.

There are times to: take authority over the devil, do warfare, bind and loosen and even see miracles happen, because of the correct kind of prayer.

Asking and receiving is one purpose of prayer, but it's definitely not the purpose of prayer, (John 16: 24). Loving, worshiping, and fellowshipping with God is your primary purpose in prayer.

Therefore- look at Matthew 6:25, *"Therefore I say unto you, do not worry about your life what you will eat or what you will drink; nor about your body, what you will put on. Is not life more than food and the body more than clothing?"*

God has commanded believers to *"seek ye first the kingdom of God, and his righteousness."* As you do, *"all these things shall be added unto you"* (Matthew 6:33). When passionately in love with God, He takes care of you - supernaturally. Living to love Him, you release powerful spiritual dynamics that positively affect the flow of provision in your life. God is the very center of your life! That does not necessarily mean you become a preacher behind a pulpit.

When your whole heart is simply "God, I love You!" you will find that He has many ways of working things out.

As you spend time with the King of kings and Lord of lords, His attitude becomes your attitude. The entire way you think changes because of His influence.

When something needs fixing let God be your Source and keep your focus on Him.

When in a bind about money, check first – that you are not doing something in the flesh. Second, once convinced you are doing what you are told to do start encouraging yourself that God is your Source. Then remember God is Faithful!

This thing called stress would not be in our lives "Same O" if we were constantly in God's presence loving and worshiping Him. We should learn not to be bothered by things, because it is just not worth it. Do not let somebody rent space in your mind because of criticism! I like that statement "Same O".

Luke 4:18 says, *"The Spirit of the Lord is upon me, because he hath [past tense—already has] anointed me."* That verse says when I write or teach I do not have to beg for His anointing because I already have it. Thank you Jesus.

We know a New Covenant prayer is supposed to be prayed in the name of Jesus. Right before Jesus died He told us, *"Up until the time, you have asked nothing in my name. Now ask and you shall receive that your joy may be full. Whatsoever you ask the Father in My name, He will give it to you."* (John 16:23, 24).

Building A New Tomorrow God's Way

Your life will become stable as you enter God's presence and primarily use prayer to love and worship Him. You will have a whole new outlook. You will think differently than those who do not love and worship Him. Prayer is entering in with praise and worship not fearfulness. We are not to focus on our unworthiness but thank Him for His goodness. We are to come boldly to His throne knowing His love is always for us. We should be praying for what is waiting for us in heaven, and that it would manifest down here NOW. Colossians 1:13 tells us to take by faith that *"Jesus has delivered us out of - the kingdom of darkness - and set us into the kingdom of light."* You see "Same O" the devil has lost his legal hold on us completely. We no longer beg God to do something or move on something. This attitude is wrong and is a religious bondage; it offends God. His job is finished and he's turned the future of his ministry over to us, the Believer. We are to demand, not arrogantly, but like a kid who knows his Father has already purchased "the stuff", to receive it. I personally can see the Father driving up my driveway to my house, "Same O". He gets out and opens this huge trunk and I see it's full. I mean full! I see myself as a kid, running out to gather up what has already been purchased for me. My job is to "take it" into my house (my temple, my body, my life). I must appropriate it as mine. When we move with God we receive what is rightfully ours and then become the vessel that is used to make someone else's miracle transpire. Let's not forget to cover it all with blessings of praise and thanksgiving!

"Same O", did you forget what all "the stuff" was? It's all the stuff you are praying about. It's healing, deliverance, prosperity, love, joy, peace, jobs and much more and God's trunk is always full. It's there to be appropriated into our lives so our joy is full. You see Jesus not only took all the wrath of God so we don't get it - that's our gift of mercy for the taking. Jesus gave us all his righteousness and God doesn't impute sin to us anymore – that's our gift of grace for the taking. He has given us Grace, and Jesus has already paid for all those good gifts we do not deserve. Let's learn how to receive them.

111

Meaning get them manifested in our lives now! That is what God wants to happen for you!

He supplies abundantly because the shed blood of Jesus Christ has purchased it on Mount Calvary - the hill called SKULL. In our skull is our brain and our "thinking cap". As a "Believer in Christ" the blood has covered our skull like it did on "the mount", crucifixion day. Our minds <u>can</u> be changed or God would not command us to renew them as in Romans 12:2, *"And do not be conformed to this world, (repent of and forget the world's traditions) but be transformed by the renewing of your mind, that you may prove what is that good and acceptable and perfect will of God".*

It is our "right believing" that makes our prayers line up with which God is pleased. For he has already supplied everything for us through the crucifixion and resurrection, thus the atonement! It is our "right believing" that causes us to receive the manifestation already purchased where the new age of Grace began two thousand years ago.

So "Same O", turn your eyes upon Jesus, look full in His wonderful face, and the things of earth will grow strangely dim in the light of His glory and grace. Those words tell it perfectly. It's a song of love by Helen H. Lemmel telling us to readjust, refocus our camera lenses and find prayer <u>primarily</u> for loving God. Our life will become stable as we enter God's presence and love and worship Him in prayer. He will give and we will find instructions and directions for our lives in those kind of prayer times - a time of communion in love.

APPLICATION

Will "Same O", that is a lot to digest. I believe it is true and will help us in our prayers if we follow through.
This chapter is expressing what I have learned from Andrew Wommack's teachings. God gave me that vision of the Father driving up the driveway.
You can learn more about prayer by buying his book "A Better Way To Pray."[1]
These tidbits from his book will get any of us started in a better direction.[1]
Prayer is believing by faith what God has already done.
So practice faith-filled payers.
Prayer is not to inform God how bad your situation is.
He already knows what you need – even before you ask!
When we learn the Word and apply the Word that God has already healed us, our body will change.
We can speak, command the symptoms to be gone-and they will evaporate!!! We thank God that all I need has been provided at Calvary.
I must speak to the problem about God,
I do not speak to God about the problem.
I command the power of God to flow.
Praying God's solution from the Word releases life,
but praying negatively and focusing on your problems only energizes and strengthens them!
We cannot ignore the statement that some of us are praying so far off we open the door for the devil to come in and do us damage.
Proverbs 18:21 says, *"Death and life are in the power of the tongue."* Your words produce either death or life even in your prayers!!!

Let us work at pleasing our Savior in prayer.
After all He has provided everything for us and
we are looking for a better tomorrow.
Let's get started and begin to renew our minds as to how to
receive the gifts already paid for by Jesus.

XVIII
Baptism in the Holy Spirit

We are to imitate Jesus. People erroneously think that Jesus was working wonders, doing miracles and living above sin because He used his divine powers that we do not have. They forget Jesus voluntarily gave up that ability and lived here as a man. It was after his anointing by the Holy Spirit (Luke 3:22) that he worked wonders not by His own power but by the power of His Father (John 14:10). Jesus, as the Son of God, set aside his deity power while living on earth (Philippians 2:7). This is exciting because that means we can copy Him. Ephesians 5:1 tells us to be imitators of God! We as a reborn child of God, filled with the same Holy Spirit as Jesus was, can do what Jesus did. In John 17:18 we are sent by Jesus into the world to live as He lived!

How can we do these things without the baptism in the Holy Spirit? We need the power that comes with the Baptism in the Spirit in order to do our part in continuing the supernatural ministry of Jesus Christ. Jesus promised us that we would do greater works than He (John 14:12). For this to happen we need the Holy Spirit in us as He was in Jesus (Acts 10:38).

The following bits and pieces are from John Juliano's teaching on the Baptism in the Holy Spirit.[1]

<u>Who is the Holy Spirit?</u> He is not a power, a force, or an energy; He is a person. As a person, He has feelings (Eph. 4:30), a mind of infinite knowledge (Romans 8:26, 27), a will, and also He speaks (Acts 13:2, John 16:13). A force or power does not have these attributes and abilities.

The Holy Spirit is called "the Spirit of Truth" (John 16:13). He loves to bless people of truth and honesty. The Holy Spirit is also called "the Comforter" (John 14:26). He communicates the comfort and healing love of the Father to our hearts, giving us encouragement, joy, and spiritual pleasure especially in times of trial and difficulty. Also known as "the Spirit of God" and "the Spirit of the Lord", the Holy Spirit is the one who gives and inspires wisdom, understanding, counsel, might, knowledge and the fear of the Lord (Isaiah 11:2).

<u>The Work of the Holy Spirit</u>

1. He convicts the world of sin, righteousness and judgment (John 16:8).
2. He guides us into all truth (John 16:13).
3. He regenerates us (John 3:5, 6).
4. He glorifies Christ (John 16:14).
5. He reveals Christ to us and in us (John 16:14, 15).
6. He is our leader - willing to lead us (Romans 8:14).
7. He sanctifies.
8. He empowers as 1 Corinthians 4:20 says, "For the kingdom of God is not in word but in power." (Acts 1:8; 1 Cor. 4:20; 1 Cor. 2:4; Matthew 10:1; Mark 16:17-18; John 14:12; 1 John 3:8b) For a born again Christian, the normal path to receiving this power involves at least the following things.
   a) The Baptism (immersion) in the Holy Spirit (Acts 1:5; John 7:37 - 39).
   b) Total dedication to God.
   c) Brokenness (Romans 7:18; John 15:56).
9. He fills us (Ephesians 5:18) (Romans 8:11; Luke 11:36).
10. He teaches us to pray (Romans 8:26, 27; 1 Cor.14:15).
11. He tells us that we are children of God (Rom. 8:16).
12. He produces in us the fruit of the Spirit (Gal. 5:22, 23).
13. He gives special supernatural gifts (I Cor. 12:8:10).

Every true Christian is born of the Spirit. It is important to state that every true born-again Christian has the Holy Spirit. *"Now if any one does not have the Spirit of Christ, he is not His."* The Holy Spirit is given by God *"to those who obey Him"* (Acts 5:32). The Holy Spirit enters our human spirit when we are born-again of the Spirit of God (John 3). Jesus comes into us by his Spirit (John 1:12). However, the dimension of power that God wants for His children can only be reached through the Baptism in the Holy Spirit. It is God's will that every Christian be baptized in the Holy Spirit (Acts 2:38, 39).

Some say that the Baptism in the Holy Spirit no longer exists today. Others take another approach and say that EVERY born again Christian was baptized in the Spirit at his conversion. Both kinds of teaching have the effect of robbing believers of something very important that Christ provided for them as part of their necessary inheritance in this life.

In the case of the apostles, the Baptism in the Spirit and being born of the Spirit were two separate events. They were born of the Spirit in John 20:22, *"And when He had said this, He breathed on them, and said to them, 'Receive the Holy Spirit'"* <u>before</u> the ascension. But they were baptized in the Spirit on the day of Pentecost <u>after</u> the ascension. It is important to note only then the promise of Mark 16:17 was fulfilled in the lives of the believers, for this began at Pentecost, *"they were all filled with the Holy Spirit and began to speak with tongues, as the Spirit gave them utterance"* (Acts 2:4).

Take Paul in the era of Grace. He received regeneration at the moment of his repentance in faith (Acts 9:3-8). Three days later, God had Ananias lay hands on Saul so that he would receive his sight and be <u>filled with the Holy Spirit</u> (Acts 9:17). Paul tells you in Corinthians *"I thank God that I speak in tongues more than you all" (1Corinthians 14:18).* Not so much in church, of course, but outside the meetings in private so as to build himself up. In this way, his preaching was both understand-able and powerful (1 Corinthians 14:19; 2:1-4).

Let us remember that <u>God did not trust the writing of the New Testament to anyone who did not speak in tongues</u>. People who despise tongues because their churches don't believe in it make the same kind of mistake as those in formal traditional churches. These reject the idea of regeneration by the Spirit at the moment of repentance and faith because it contradicts the long-held dogma of the church. The Bible, "Same O", must settle the issue - not our traditions, theologies and lack of experience. The Bible says *"Desire earnestly to prophesy, and do <u>not</u> forbid to speak with tongues." (1 Corinthians 14:39)*

The Scripture further shows that it is always desirable and God's will for people to be filled with the Holy Spirit in such a way as to be clothed with the power of God and to speak with other tongues (Ephesians 5:18; I Corinthians 14:5a). The main purpose of the Baptism of the Holy Spirit in this life is to give us more power to demonstrate Christ and win people to Him, so that they can be saved (Acts 1:8).

"Same O" when you seek deeper relationship in God there is much more promised to you, the Believer! It comes with submission to the Word of God and to the Holy Spirit. We must trust God's Spirit to lead us in our battle with the world, the flesh and the Devil. That is why there are three types of tongues.

1. Praying in tongues from man to God: for private edification, prayer and praise to God. This requires no interpretation (1 Cor. 14:2).
2. Prophecies in tongues with interpretation (1 Cor. 14:5-9). These are messages in tongues from God to man. They require interpretation in most cases.
3. In the case of when a speaker is saying (by the spirit) words in a native language that are understood by the hearers but not by himself, it can be said tongues are a sign for the unbelieving (Acts 2:8; 1Cor. 14:22).

Speaking in tongues helps us to train our spirits to hear the voice of God and to operate in the other gifts of the Holy Spirit (1Cor.12:8-10). Especially, "Same O" for us in the Western culture, who have trained ourselves to base all our speaking, thinking and actions on reasoning that we can understand. The area where God speaks to us first is in our spirits. Our spirits are the part of us through which we hear the voice of God. It is <u>not</u> through rational processes or deductions that we arrive at what God is saying. We do not arrive at the experiential knowledge of God through philosophy (1 Corinthians 1:21), but through revelation by the Holy Spirit.

"The promise is for you...." (Acts 2:39). What is the promise? It is the gift of the Holy Spirit (Acts 2:38). *"It shall come to pass in the last days, says God. That I will pour forth of My Spirit upon all flesh; Your sons and your daughters shall prophesy, Your young men shall see visions, Your old men shall dream dreams"* (Acts 2:17). Before *"the last days"* the Holy Spirit was only poured out upon specially chosen servants of God, especially prophets, priests and kings. On this side of the cross the Bible teaches us, all Christians are royal priests (1 Peter 2:9). The Holy Spirit can be poured out on all mankind (Acts 2:17), so this certainly includes you. The applicable time period for the promise, the last days, is the time between Christ's ascension and second coming. The last days are not over yet as Acts 2:19-20 has not yet been fulfilled. Therefore the promise is still fully applicable to all believers today. Yes, today God pours forth of His Spirit upon <u>all</u> mankind.[1]

Yes, "Same O" those last days are now. It is the time between Christ's ascension and His second coming. Acts 2:19-20 has not happened. The last days aren't over. The great and awesome day of the Lord is when He comes back for us and raptures us off this planet. Many, many Christians are talking about the FOUR BLOOD MOONS today 10.10.2013. (You can look it up in Joel 2:30-31 and on www.jhm.org).[2] The promise is still ours. The following is how to receive the Baptism in the Holy Spirit for the Believer to have power like Jesus. To carry on and imitate Jesus. To finish His ministry is our ministry! Praise His Name.

Suggested Prayer to Ask for the Baptism in the Holy Spirit

Dear Jesus, thank you for the most wonderful gift of all - the gift of salvation. Lord, you promised another gift, the gift of the Holy Spirit. I want all you have for me. Baptize me in the Holy Spirit like in the early church. I consecrate my life to you. I am a believer and you said that believers would speak in unknown languages (tongues). Give me now this gift of tongues. I believe I receive the power that I have asked for and can do what Jesus wants me to do. Thank you Jesus!

Now concentrate on Jesus. Your step of faith here is to open your mouth and make syllables you don't understand. Stay with it until you are drenched in His Spirit speaking a new language.[3]

Trust that the Holy Spirit within you will control what you say. It's a language for prayer and praise!

The Holy Spirit wants us to continue to <u>meditate on the Word</u> and on good things (Philippians 4:8). Stay close to Him in a wonderful relationship, and then the purpose of the Baptism in the Holy Spirit will be achieved in our lives to carry out and finish the ministry that Jesus started while here on earth. We will be able to do that which He did. Yes, we will be imitating Him! That will bring us into a brand new tomorrow - God's Way! Praise the Lord!

APPLICATION[4]

Repentance
Necessary for salvation (Acts 17:30, Luke 13:3, Acts 2:28).
Examine yourself
Decide to live for God wholeheartedly.
Confess and forsake your sin trusting Jesus for forgiveness
(1 John 1:9).

.Renounce Evil Power
Renounce any dabbling you have done with the occult
(including astrology).
Renounce the evil power now in Jesus' name.
If in doubt about something, renounce it too (Rom. 14:23).

Thirst After God
You must speak, trusting God to give the language. Do not worry about understanding the sounds you make - it's according to the language the Holy Spirit gives you.
Keep speaking in tongues, allowing the Holy Spirit to flood your spirit, soul, and body, <u>drenching</u> you in His Presence.
Keep receiving until you are drenched!!

Ask In Faith
"Until now you have asked nothing in My name. Ask, and you will receive that your joy may he full." John 16:24

Drink
"For by one Spirit we were all baptized into one body – whether Jews or Greeks, whether slaves or free – and have all been made to drink into one Spirit."
1 Corinthians 12:13

Receive

"Therefore He who supplies the Spirit to you and works miracle among you, does He do it by the works of the Law, or by the hearing of faith?" Galatians 3:5

"Therefore I say to you, whatever things you ask when you pray, believe that you receive them, and you will have them. Mark 11:24

Yield to God an Active Thing

"For if I pray in a tongue, my spirit prays, but my understanding is unfruitful."
1Corinthians 14:14

XIX
The Sovereignty of God

God is sovereign to His Word. God has told his family, born-again believers, to imitate Jesus! Ephesians 5:1 says, *"Therefore be imitators of God as dear children."* We must understand Jesus operated on this planet earth as a man, like you and I have to operate. He did <u>not</u> act out of his divinity! Philippians 2:7 says, *"but made Himself of no reputation, taking the form of a bond-servant, and coming in the likeness of men."* Think about this "Same O", if Jesus acted out of His divinity we would not have been commanded to imitate him. There would be <u>no</u> way that we could!

Knowing we are born again and that we have the Spirit of God in us, we have the privilege to renew our minds and follow through with what God tells us "to do" in His Word. Water baptism by immersion and taking communion are a vital part of a true Christian's growth. In Peter's sermon, after Jesus went back to heaven, said in Acts 2:14 - 47 that people must: repent, be baptized and receive the gift of the Holy Spirit. Verse 42 says, *"…continue steadfastly in the apostle's doctrine and fellowship, in the breaking of bread and in prayers"*. These are all a part of following in Jesus' footsteps. Matthew 3:11 says, *"I indeed baptize you with water unto repentance, but He who is coming after me* (That is John the Baptist talking.) *is mightier than I, whose sandals I am not worthy to carry.* (He is referring to Jesus the man from Galilee, the baby born in a manger in Bethlehem of a virgin - the seed of David.) *He will baptize you with the Holy Spirit and fire"* This tells us there is a second experience of receiving the power of the Holy Spirit.

Look at these verses "Same O". They tell us why we should be able to do what Jesus did and it's all because his Word is a covenant and He won't alter His Word! Psalm 9:34 *"My covenant I will not break, nor alter the word that has gone out of my lips."*

Luke 24:49 says, *"Behold, I send the promise of My Father upon you; but tarry in the city of Jerusalem until you are endued with power from on high."*

Acts 1:8 says, *"But you shall receive power when the Holy Spirit has come upon you; and you shall be witnesses to Me in Jerusalem and in all Judea and Samaria and to the end of the earth."* 2 Peter 1:3 & 4 says, *"as His divine power has given to us all things that pertain to life and godliness through the knowledge of Him who called us by glory and virtue, by which have been given to us exceedingly great and precious promises, that through these you may be partakers of the divine nature, having escaped the corruption that is in the world through lust.* Colossians 2:9 & 10 says, *"For in Him dwells all the fullness of the Godhead bodily; and you are complete in Him, who is the head of all principality and power."*

The "power" is given to us by the baptism of Holy Spirit, with speaking in tongues, to move and do like Jesus. Without this power of God flowing through us we can't be the kind of lord we're meant to be. Jesus is the KING we are the little kings. Jesus is LORD, we are the little lords. These "kings" and "lords" do the business of thee Lord. 1 Timothy 6:15 says, " (Jesus Christ's appearing) *will manifest in His own time, He who is the blessed and only Potentate (sovereign), the King of kings and Lord of lords."*

Do you see, we the TRUE CHURCH has been given a job "to do" and it is to finish Jesus' ministry in the here and now until He comes back to gather his entire family to Him. We have to be able to do "like Jesus did" or we'll never continue his ministry.

Mark 16:15-18 tells us the following. Jesus said to them, *"Go into all the world and preach the gospel to every creature. He who believes and is baptized will be saved: but he who does not believe will be condemned. And these signs will follow those who believe: In My name they will cast out demons; they will speak with new tongues; they will take up serpents; and if they drink anything deadly it will by no means hurt them. They will lay hands on the sick, and they will recover."* After he said this "Same O" he was received up into heaven, and Jesus sat down at the right hand of God. Then the disciples took over His ministry and went out into the world.

God needs us to bind up the evil today and go forth boldly as ambassadors for Jesus. God can't. He has given all power that was originally given to Adam and stolen by the 'evil one' in the Garden of Eden, back to us (mankind) through the death, burial and resurrection of Jesus. God is a Spirit that needs to reside in you (mankind) and thus "man" goes in confidence to imitate Jesus. That's how God does "stuff" today. God won't break that covenant that He has spoken and given to us.

God has given us everything we need to do the job. As you study and meditate on the Word which is a positive life source, you grow in His Grace. John 15:7 says, *"If ye abide in me, and my words abide in you, ye shall ask what ye will, and it shall be done unto you."* One reason we, the Believers, are so short on power is that we don't have the true revelation of Colossians 3:16, *"Let the word of Christ dwell in you richly..."* We are growing "Same O"! Yes, we are!

Once we are saved, baptized in the Holy Spirit, and have humbly surrendered our lives to our Lord, "we can" do a lot to honor Jesus.

- We can renew our minds to things above.
- We can walk in faith.
- We can share the Good News Gospel.
- We can talk to our Father.
- We can expect good things daily.
- We can receive blessings and favor daily.
- We can receive power from above.
- We can heal the sick. We're the vessel, He is the power.
- We can change the rotten weather headed our way.
- We can cast out demons.
- We can prosper.

- We can have joy unspeakable.
- We can love unconditionally.
- We can have peace.
- We can have self-control (temperance).
- We can have patience (long suffering).
- We can show kindness (gentleness).
- We can have faith and mix it with the promises that are ours to overcome.
- We can be humble (meek and gentle).
- We can have goodness in our lives.
- We can forgive.
- We can forget.
- We can succeed.

This is just a <u>tiny list</u> of all that Jesus purchased for his family.

God is sovereign to His Word.
What Jesus did we can do!
He calmed the storms – so should we.
He healed the sick – so should we.
He did miracles – so should we.
He taught the Word – so should we.
He had compassion for all people – so should we.
We are told to imitate Jesus – so we should.
To get things done God works through people.
He does not work magic.
He does work miracles through his imitators.
Jesus did <u>not</u> use his divinity here on the earth.
Jesus is our example to follow.
Jesus talked to the Father and found out where, what and when to act.
We are supposed to talk to our Father and find out where,
what and when to act.
That is doing it the same way Jesus did.

We are to reign on this earth above the carnal man's way. Jesus has paid for it all - it's ours for the taking. Jesus <u>wants</u> us to receive all he paid for. He <u>wants</u> us to fulfill his ministry. That's why He commanded us to GO in His name which is above every name.

Philippians 2:9 ways *"Therefore God also has highly exalted Him* (Jesus) *and given Him the name which is above every name."* In His name we can go because we are the modern day disciples and Jesus is saying to us, "You can" so - "GO"!

In Matthew 28:18 we read *"All authority has been given to Me in heaven and on earth. Go therefore and make disciples of all the nations, baptizing them in the name of the Father and of the Son and of the Holy Spirit, teaching them to observe all things that I have commanded you: and lo, I am with you always, even to the end of the age."*

The end of the age means the end of the dispensation of the Acts of the Holy Ghost which is the dispensation of Grace. It's going to end "Same O" and that'll be when Jesus comes back. Until then we "GO".

APPLICATION

Jesus corrected the "Fall" and has given us, the "Born-Again Christian," the power and privilege to "GO" and do for Jesus until he comes back for his own. God needs us to work on behalf of Jesus. Remember, rather than praying "God please stop the storm" we need to speak a <u>command</u> from your mouth "Peace be still."

God is sovereign to the way He has set up His kingdom. We must follow His lead on how He has set it up for it to work in our lives. God needs you to speak in boldness and he'll use you, the vessel. He will pour his supernatural power through you to the problem or situation with victory as fruit. The one who has mixed their faith with the Word promise has the resultant overcoming power and victory is manifested from on high. That's probably the longest sentence in the book with wrong grammar, but it's right biblically.

Its message is truth! God is sovereign to His Word.

Jesus I can't help but love you, to think you desire "Same O", the reader and myself to help you build your kingdom till Jesus comes back. Jesus is coming back and I'll share more about that
in the chapter, "Tell Them I Am Coming!"

Remember God doesn't lie, you can bank your life on what He says.
<u>You can literally book your life on what God says.</u>
That book is the Lamb's Book of life found in Revelation 21:27.
Those who have been reached by the ones that "GO" will find their names written in that Lamb's Book of Life.
There is great security in a Sovereign God! He's not fickle.
He is the same yesterday, today and forever (Hebrews 13:8).
Malachi 3:6 says, *"For I am the Lord, I do not change..."*

XX
Believers Have the Mind of Christ

Jesus knew everything he needed to know for His daily walk because He always talked to His Father. His Father told him what was up. Since we are to imitate Jesus we need to know how to get information from God just like Jesus did. "When you accept Jesus Christ as your Savior, the moment you are born again, that moment God imparts to you Righteousness. That gives you a standing in the presence of the Father identical with the standing of Jesus." If that is an offence to you, take it up with E.W. Kenyon because he said it first.[1] If we know we are the righteousness of God, we know we have the mind of Christ in us. 1 Corinthians 2:16 says, *"For who hath known the mind of the Lord, that he may instruct him? But, we have the mind of Christ."* The problem is, how do I get it to work in situations where I need help. This is where the rubber meets the road, especially if you are not in agreement with the Word concerning speaking in tongues. God does not expect us to do the works of Jesus and to be holy as He is holy without having available to us the same measure of the Holy Spirit as Jesus had. Now, how does that work? The Baptism in the Spirit is an essential part of all this.

When the manifestation of the gifts of the spirit are available for you as: wisdom, knowledge, faith, healing, miracles, tongues, interpretation, prophecy, and discernment of spirits, you are free to use them to help in a time of need. This can be a need of and for yourself or for ministry to somebody else. When you have this gift you can pray in tongues and receive the answer, either in your heart or through interpretation. Romans 8:26-27 says, *"Likewise the Spirit also helpeth our infirmities: for we know not what we should pray for as we ought: but the Spirit itself maketh intercession for us with groanings which cannot be uttered. And God that searcheth the hearts knoweth what is the mind of the Spirit, because the Holy Spirit maketh intercession for the saints according to the will of God."* The Holy Spirit takes hold together with us in prayer. The Holy Spirit does not automatically do it and we cannot do it on our own. You start in your feeble effort and the Holy Spirit intercedes through you. Both together helps us overcome the problems in our lives. The Baptism of the Holy Spirit that includes tongues is of tremendous importance in being able to receive your answer. So He that searches the hearts, knows the mind of the Spirit. You got that, "Same O"? We are moving forward!

Let the Spirit take over and then you have perfect communication between you and God. 1 John 2:20 says, *"But ye have an unction from the Holy One, and ye know all things." KJV* Think about that "Same O." We really do have it all (the fullness of God like Adam did before he fell.) in our own spirit when born again. We are learning to draw it out of our spirit. Let's read 1 John 2:27 *"But the anointing which ye have received of him abideth in you, and ye need not that any man teach you: but as the same anointing teacheth you of all things, and is truth, and is no lie, and even as it hath taught you, ye shall abide in him." KJV*

So we have established that the mind of Christ is in your spirit not in your brain. 1 Corinthians 2:16 has told us that very plainly. It says, *"For 'who has known the mind of the Lord that he may instruct Him?' But we have the mind of Christ".* God has given us this and we need to know that it is there and we need to be able to release it. Now to draw it out you pray in tongues. That is like sticking a bucket down into your spirit and drawing out the mind of Christ. When you speak in tongues you speak in mysteries. When you speak in tongues it is your spirit that knows all things not your brain. When praying in tongues you are praying the supernatural hidden mysteries of God. The next step is to ask for the interpretation and you will have your answer to the problem or situation before you.

1 Corinthians 14:13 says, *"Therefore let him who speaks in a tongue pray that he may interpret."* Isn't God good!

We must learn to fine-tune our spirits enough to pick up the voice of the Spirit. We pick up on a few things but we do fade in and out. We don't stay on God's wave length all the time. So as we continue to pray in the spirit we adjust our 'spiritual tuner'! When we pray in other tongues it is the most effective and fastest method to tune into God. Praying in tongues (praying in the spirit) we are not praying our thoughts and plans but rather His thoughts and plans. You speak mysteries when praying in tongues. You are calling forth parts of God's plan we don't understand. You are praying the perfect will of God. God knows how to help us in our daily walk. He can give us direction and deliver his people if we get our hearts in tune with the Spirit. I heard it said this way. If we will get our minds and hearts in tune with what God's doing, there will be an explosion of the power of God that will turn our lives around and this world around. "Same O", that statement should challenge us to pray in other tongues unceasingly.

APPLICATION

OH, how God loves you and me! Do you feel His Presence? Think about what he has supplied for His people to help them out in life. God's no dummy. He has planned lots of things to help us in our questions and troubles of life. He desires for us to be His overcomers. The gift of the Baptism of the Holy Spirit is essential to draw out the hidden mysteries of the mind of Christ hidden in our spirit.

I have given you a teaching on how to receive the <u>Baptism of the Holy Spirit</u> in a previous chapter.

Go back over it if you skipped it, it is so important.

I pray, *"That your faith should not stand in the wisdom of men, but in the power of God"* 1 Corinthians 2:5.

Be like Paul from now on. Paul said, *"I thank my God, I speak with tongues more than you all."*

"Same O" we must receive the Baptism of the Holy Spirit and use it, praying unceasingly.

This man had to shift from a legalistic and law-minded heathen to a born-again man. He went into Arabia for three years to hear God on why the Law was outdated, and if so what next. He received the revelation knowledge through the Holy Spirit and wrote a major portion of the New Testament.

This revelation knowledge experience is just as much for us today as it was for Paul. Paul lived in the era or dispensation of the Holy Spirit called GRACE and so are we. It was this Grace that God spoke about and explained to Paul, so therefore we too can experience all that is ours in Christ Jesus and then reach out to others in our daily walk. We today will be writing the bible in the sense that the book of Acts is not finished. There is not an amen at the end of Acts like the other books.

The church is still writing and writing and writing, using the mind of Christ to build up His Kingdom of Love.

XXI

Money

Paul tells us something about money in Philippians 4:17. It states, *"Not because I desire a gift: but I desire fruit that may abound to your account."* Did you know you have a bank account in heaven if you are born again? My question to you "Same O", is how do you get anything in it? And for what reason do I want anything in it? The Bible says in Proverbs 3:9 *"Honor the Lord with thy substance, and with the first fruits of all thine increase."* I am going to share a few verses that will set our hearts toward the delights of God's heart.

Matthew 6:19-21 says, *"Lay not up for yourselves treasures upon earth, where moth and rust doth corrupt, and where thieves break through and steal: but lay up for yourselves treasures in heaven, where neither moth nor rust doth corrupt, and where thieves do not break through nor steal: For where your treasure is, there will your heart be also."* Now if you want to learn something about yourself look at your checkbook. That will show you very clearly where your dollars are spent, right "Same O"? Check it out and see where your heart is! Luke 6:38 says, *"Give, and it will be given unto you; good measure, pressed down, shaken together, and running over will be put into your bosom. For with the same measure that you use, it will be measured back to you."* You give to God and then pressing, shaking, and running over, men will give back to you. You see God uses people to give back to you. It is not going to fall out of the sky. Let us be sure when we give, it is of and for somebody that stands up for Jesus and His attributes. That is putting treasure in your bank. Just giving to a secular "hope chest in the town" may put your gift at risk. Yes, Galatians 6:7 tells us *"Be not deceived; God is not mocked: for whatsoever a man soweth, that shall he also reap."* If you give sparingly you will receive sparingly. This verse tells us we can give in many ways besides monetarily. Let us look at Matthew 10:8, *"Heal the sick, cleanse the lepers, raise the dead, cast out devils: freely ye have received, freely give."* KJV Yes, there are many services you can do "as unto the Lord" that will build your account up wonderfully while honoring your Lord.

Let us look at Matthew 16:21 which is the story of the rich young ruler. He asked Jesus *"what good thing shall I do, that I may have eternal life?"* You know by now "Same O" that you cannot earn your way into heaven by <u>doing</u> something. This ruler thought he could. Jesus said to him, *"...if thou wilt enter into life, keep the commandments."* The guy asked Jesus, "Which?" This guy is not thinking clearly. Jesus tells him a list of them and then the rich young ruler says, *"I have kept them from my youth up: what lack I yet?"* Does he really think he kept them? Jesus ignores his arrogance and tells him *"...go sell that thou hast, and give to the poor, and thou shalt have treasure in heaven: and come and follow me."* This guy missed an opportunity of a lifetime. He did not respond correctly. He thought giving away his life treasure for Jesus meant a negative balance for him. He could not see that in God's Kingdom you give to receive. He had a natural eye, a carnal eye that could not look into God's treasure account of abundance. This man missed it financially and eternally. I hope he met Jesus another time and opened up his tight fist to honor God and receive all that Jesus offered him. Remember Proverbs 9:20-21 *"I lead in the way of righteousness, that I may cause those that love me to inherit substance; and I will fill their treasures."* Jesus wants us to prosper, he paid the price for it on the cross. Prosperity was included in the atonement.

The following are bits and pieces from Jerry Savelle's September 2013 letter. "What you believe about tithing, sowing, and reaping has the potential to block God's blessing or it can position you to receive an abundant harvest. Tithing and giving was in place before the Law was given, commanded during the Law, and encouraged after the Law.

Genesis 8:22 says, *'while the earth remains, seedtime and harvest... shall not cease'.*[1] Did you get that? God said that 'It shall not cease!' "God makes it very clear that its duration is for as long as the earth remains. The earth is still here so, 'seedtime and harvest' are yet to be practiced even by New Testament believers that live under grace." That is us "Same O"!! We can cash in on this blessing yet today. No pun intended! We just need a different attitude than those living in the time of Law or before. "Tithing is no longer a debt that I owe but a seed that I sow. In 1 Corinthians Paul wrote *'Now concerning the collection...you must do also on the first day of the week...'* indicates that receiving offerings was a vital part of their worship. Tithing and giving for us, who live in the era of Grace is not about works or fulfilling the Law. Tithing is not some religious obligation to me-it is an act of love. We give as a doer of the Word (see James1:22). 'God so loved He gave.' Paul tells us in 2 Corinthians 9:6 *'But this I say: He who sows sparingly will also reap sparingly, and he who sows bountifully will also reap bountifully.'* Verse 8, says, *'And God is able to make all grace abound toward you...'* Our giving is divinely linked to 'God's grace abounding' in our lives. We know that grace and favor are synonymous. So, if we use the word favor here, then he is saying that God's favor abounds in our lives when we are regular and consistent givers and sowers."

"Same O", have you ever read the story in the bible about Elijah and the widow of Zarephath. It is found in I Kings 17. When God gave the prophet Elijah (a man of God) a word - he boldly went to the King and told him the message. Sounds simple enough! Did you know the King was on a man hunt to kill all the prophets at that time? It took courage, faith, and boldness to speak the Word of God to the King. Elijah owned the WORD (he took it to heart) - he knew it was God and moved on it in obedience. Skipping most of the story, and moving forward to where the ravens bought food to Elijah at the brook of Cherith, we find the brook dried up. Elijah waited for another WORD from God. God told him He had commanded a widow woman to sustain him at Zarephath, I Kings 17:9. This widow had heard God in her own home, in the land of no rain for many years. Her cupboard had one meal left for her son and herself. This woman had heard the voice of God once and heard she was to feed a prophet. Out picking up sticks for the last meal of her life she meets Elijah. Elijah calls to her *"Please bring me a little water in a cup that I may drink, and as she went Elijah said, Please bring me a morsel of bread in your hand."* The widow replies, *"I only have a hand full of flour...and a little oil left....I was picking up sticks to bake it, eat it and die."* Elijah gave another WORD of God, *"Do not fear, go and do ... make me a small cake first... and afterwards make some for yourself...for the Lord God said...your flour and jar of oil will not dry up until the Lord sends rain... So she went away and did according to the word of Elijah..."* She served the "man of God" first and her vat of oil never stopped running over *"according to the word of the Lord which He spoke by Elijah"*, I Kings 17:9-16. If the life of this woman doesn't validate Luke 6:30 I do not know what does! *"Give, and it will be given to you: good measure, pressed down, shaken together, and running over <u>will be put into your bosom</u>."* The prophet showed her how to receive, she by faith responded with a heart towards God and she was blessed.

"Same O", if we who are "in Christ Jesus" would respond to the WORD of God in obedience like this widow woman did we would find "the rules of God's Kingdom are well worth obeying. We must step out of the natural and into the supernatural by faith to receive our rewards in the here and now! Remember Mark 10:29-30 where Jesus said, *"assuredly, I say to you, there is no one who has left house or brothers or sisters or father or mother or wife or children or lands; for My sake and the gospel's, who shall not receive a hundredfold NOW in this time - houses and brothers and sisters and mothers and children and lands, with persecutions--and in the age to come, eternal life."*

That, "Same O", is a pretty good reason to be obedient to God and His Word! We just don't get it how badly God wants to bless us. I remember what Jerry Savelle said: "The blessing of God on our lives empowers us to prosper, but the favor of God on our lives is what produces the opportunities for it to happen. Our regular and consistent tithing, giving, and sowing increases our opportunities for prosperity." That will change the "same o" "same o" in our lives', <u>**if**</u> we follow through with God's teaching.

APPLICATION

Learn to pray about your giving,
do not just give on a hype or under an emotional whim.
Give as God directs.
"Never confuse works and grace.
We are saved by grace and grace alone!
It is the finished work of Jesus that gives us right standing with God.
The Bible is true, you will reap what you sow.
Tithing and sowing positions you for more of God's
favor and blessing!" [2]
Do the WORD and Favor and Blessing from God
will improve your life!
A sower is <u>never</u> without seed.
"Same O" if you want change, get out that checkbook
and see where you have fallen short
with your <u>change</u>.

XXII

Healing

Our redeemer's blood is our healing factor, "Same O". Disease is a part of the curse! Disease is the physical penalty of iniquity. The "Great Exchange" is that sin and sickness have passed from me to Calvary - salvation and health have passed from Calvary to me. God removed the curse justly by substitution. Because Christ bore in His body all our physical liabilities on account of sin, our bodies are released judicially from disease. The Israelites ate their first Passover Lamb on the run. It gave them physical life and strength as they <u>were</u> worn out and poorly fed for 400 years. Our Passover Lamb shows up at the Lord's Supper and as we partake of Christ we are keeping his death and benefits before us. In Christ we have both physical and spiritual life, and this is "ours" once we're born again. The Israelites ate flesh of the Passover Lamb for physical strength. It shows that we also, receive physical life and strength from Christ (1 Corinthians 11:29, 5:7 & 11:30). Through the Fall we lost everything. Jesus recovered it all through His atonement. Jesus bore our sicknesses and pain. Isaiah 53:4 denotes actual substitution. That verse means "to lift up, to bear away, to convey, or to remove in a distance." It is a Levitical word, and is applied to the scapegoat that bore away the sins of the people. Yes, it denotes actual substitution and a complete removal of the thing borne. Praise the Lord for that!

The bearing of, and removal of human disease is an integral part of the vicarious atonement. That is our healing. Jesus is the Savior of the body as well as the spirit. He comes to make His blessings flow far as the curse is found. Every born-again person is in covenant with God. His name is Jehovah-Rapha which translated means "I Am the Lord thy Physician" or "I am the Lord that healeth thee". Disease is the incipient death that entered the world by sin. Disease entered by sin, and its remedy is found in the Redeeming Christ. Jehovah-Rapha never changed His name.

In the Old Testament there are "types" of the atonement given as in Leviticus 14:8 - the priest is atoning for the leper. If in the Old Testament times the priest could atone for the leper. Why can't Jesus our high priest atone for our sickness in this era of Grace? Our covenant is a "better covenant." Hebrews 8:6 says, *"...He has obtained a more excellent ministry, in as much as He is also mediator of a better covenant, which was established on better promises."*

> Through the Fall, Adam lost everything.
> Jesus recovered all through His Atonement.

When Jesus talked about the year of Jubilee, all possessions were to be returned to every man. In our era of Grace that includes forgiveness and healing. Jesus is still healing all who come to Him by <u>living</u> faith.

> God forgives by the atonement of Jesus Christ.
> God heals disease by the atonement of Jesus Christ.

How can we do "greater things" if we don't include healing for our body and soul? It was a major part of Jesus' ministry! Jesus went to the cross: spirit, soul, and body. Christ was born under the law to redeem us from it. Christ was made a curse (Galatians 3:13) and redeemed us from all sickness and disease. If the body was not included in redemption, how can there be a resurrection? Why shouldn't the 'last Adam' take away all the 'first Adam' brought upon us? The power of God can only be claimed where the will of God is known. Our living faith must rest on the will of God alone, not our desires or wishes or feelings! No one ever appealed in vain to Jesus for healing as recorded in the Holy Bible. Healing is for all! "A living church is one in which the living Christ lives and walks, doing through its members what He did in the days of His flesh. It must be a healing church as well as a soul-saving church." James Moore Hickson pleads. "Healing is provided by the atonement and is a part of the Gospel, which Christ commands us to preach."[1]

Christ's ministry continues through his believers in "His Church". Jesus healed people because of His love and compassion for all mankind. Acts 1:1 says Jesus *"began to do and teach what was to be continued"*. Jesus left so the Holy Spirit could come; that increased His ministry. The early church took Christ at His word and prayed in union for signs and wonders - until the place shook. The Holy Spirit came to execute for us all the blessings purchased by Christ's redemption and pledged by the seven redemptive names. It was the Holy Spirit who worked all the miracles of healing at the hands of Jesus Christ. Jesus never undertook a miracle until in an answer to His prayer, the Holy Spirit, the Miracle Worker, came upon Him; and in full release of the Spirit He cast out demons and healed the sick.

[My Note: Jesus is our example. Eph. 5:1 says, *"Therefore be imitators of God as dear children."* Andrew Wommack says in his book "You've Already Got It" on page 186 that "Jesus didn't know all things in His human mind."[1] Jesus operated in life here like we have to do things. He had to pray to His Father and through His Baptism of the Holy Spirit, Acts 10:38, Jesus would receive direction and power and then do what his Father needed done. (Mark 14:36). He was obedient to his Father. Yes, Jesus is our example.][2]

Hasn't modern theology robbed the Holy Spirit of part of His ministry? Divine healing is not unconditionally promised to all Christians regardless of their conduct. It's for those who believe and obey (Ps. 25:10). Remember *"The Son of God was manifested, that he might destroy the works of the devil" (John 3:8)*. Salvation is all-inclusive of: deliverance, preservation, healing, health and soundness. Are all who have been baptized washed from all their sins? NO! But those who have faith are; and what water is in the ordinance of Christian baptism, so is the ordinance of anointing to the sick for healing.

The age of miracles is not past. *"The Lord is gracious, and full of compassion; slow to anger, and of great mercy. The Lord is good to all: and his tender mercies are over all his work." Psalm 145:8-9*. God is love. It's faith in His love and His willingness to bless that secures His blessings! The "sick" need to know the Lord is gracious, not just able but willing! (Matthew 8:3). Actually He *"delighteth in mercy"* (Micah 7:18). God has a benevolent heart. If you want to please Him "Same O" move the obstacles out of the way of the exercise of His benevolence. We are to place ourselves where God's mercy can reach us without His having to violate the glorious principles of His moral government. Then, wait and see if you don't experience the most overwhelming demonstration of His love and mercy. The blessings will flow until you have reached the limit of your expectation. Jesus' departure was to open the way for His compassion to be manifested on a much larger scale. John 16:7 says, *"Nevertheless I tell you the truth; it is to your advantage that I go away for if I do not go away, the Helper will not come to you; but if I depart, I will send Him to you."*

Christ's compassion towards the sick has not been modified or withdrawn since his exaltation. We must not take any position that veils and interferes with the manifestation of the greatest attribute of Deity, God's compassion, which is divine love in action. Jesus' face was set like a flint" (Isaiah 50:7) refused the most natural impulse of His soul to instantly pray for twelve legions of angels to enable Him to escape the agony of the cross (Matthew 26: 53-54). Then there would have been only a judgment seat, and no mercy seat, for fallen man with all his needs of body, soul and spirit. He was then and is now, moved by compassion toward all who need Him as the One who is: Ever Present, Peace, Shepherd, Provider, Victor, Righteousness and Physician, these are the seven blessings secured by the tragedy of the Cross, and revealed to us by His seven redemptive names. He's still <u>full of mercy (compassion)</u>.[3] Ps. 86:5 says, *"For You, Lord, are good and ready to forgive. And abundant in mercy to all those who call upon You."*

APPROPRIATING BODILY HEALING
STEP ONE

The next notes give you a complete foundation for faith to manifest your healing for today. There are three steps given.

1. The Bible clearly teaches that it is God's will to heal until the allotted span of life is complete, Exodus 23:25-26.
2. Be <u>fully convinced</u> by the Word of God that your healing is the will of God.
3. Faith begins where the will of God is known. Faith for healing must rest on the will of God alone not your desires, wishes, or feelings (symptoms).
4. People must not talk ten words against healing and one word in favor of it.
5. Faith is expecting God to do His will. God intends for us to pray in faith.
6. Through the atonement of Christ, both salvation and bodily healing were provided.
7. Jesus healed all diseases on the ground of the Atonement, (Matt. 8:17), as Moses healed in the types of Leviticus 14 and 15 through the Atonement.

Building A New Tomorrow God's Way

8. Jesus healed them all, NO exceptions, because in His coming Atonement, *"Himself took our infirmities and bore our sickness"*, Matthew 8:17.
9. What Calvary provides is for <u>all</u>!
10. God's way of saving a soul, of healing the body, or anything else is He sends His Word - sends His Promise - and keeps the promise wherever it produces faith, Psalms 107:20, 1 Thessalonians 2:13, Proverbs 4:22. Our faith *"cometh by hearing"*, Romans 10:17.
11. We must see the Creator and Redeemer of the body as its physician before we have reason to expect healing.
12. His seven redemptive names reveal what our redemption includes. Seven is a perfect number that covers the whole scope of human needs. The meaning follows His name.

Jehovah - Shammah	---	Ever Present (Ezek. 48:85) (Ephesians. 2:13)
Jehovah - Ra-ah	---	Shepherd (Ps. 23:11) (John 10:11, 15)
Jehovah - Shalom	---	Peace (Isaiah 53.5)
Jehovah - Jireh	---	Provider (Genesis 22:8)
Jehovah - Nissi	---	Victor (Colossians 2:15)
Jehovah – Tsidkenu	---	Righteousness (Jeremiah 23:6)
Jehovah - Raphe	---	Physician (Exodus 15:26) (Matthew 8:17)

13. The scriptures say, *"If a man therefore purge himself from these (iniquities), he shall be a vessel unto honour, sanctified and meet for the master's use, and prepared unto every good work" 2 Tim 2:21*. We cannot be *"prepared unto every good work"* while we are sick in bed. God's new covenant provides that we each will be made *"perfect in every good work to do his will"* (Heb. 13:21)[4]

That's the Good News - too good to be true!! But it's TRUE!!

APPROPRIATING BODILY HEALING
STEP TWO

1. Be sure you are right with God because our redemptive blessings are conditional.
2. When seeking healing for our bodies, there should be no compromise with the adversary of our souls, for he is the author of our disease.
3. We must settle all questions of obedience to God, or we're not on blessing ground.
4. There's something wrong when you desire the blessing but not the Blesser.
5. God is waiting to say to Satan and disease what he said to Pharaoh: "Let my people go, that they may serve me."
6. When you delight in the Lord, then he gives you the desires of your heart (Psalms 37:4).
7. A spiritual law of Faith is: The union of our hearts and wills with God's will and purpose, and where this unity is lacking results are impossible!
8. It's the Spirit in me that does the quickening. If you need a miracle, get in touch with the Miracle Worker. You must elbow out of the way, and press beyond: selfishness, disobedience, unconfessed sins, luke warmness, public opinion, tradition of men, articles written against divine healing. In fact you must often press beyond your own pastor, who may not be unenlightened in this part of the Gospel. In fact you must often press beyond doubts, double mindedness, symptoms, feelings, and the lying serpent.

God is waiting to pour out the Holy Spirit in fullness upon us. He comes as Christ's Executive to execute for us all the blessings provided by Calvary which pledged to us His seven redemptive and covenant names. All that is in the vine, including both spiritual and physical life, belongs to us – the branches.[5]

APPROPRIATING HEALING BLESSINGS
STEP THREE

1. Believe God has provided healing for you for now - that's His first move.
2. It's our move now: We must expect what He promises when we pray. This will cause us to act on our faith before we see the healing, because healing comes in the next move, which is God's move. God never moves out of turn!

Remember, Noah was *"warned of God of things not seen yet"* (Hebrews11:7). His move was to believe that the flood was coming and to act on his faith by building the ship on dry land. Therefore, when God says to *"any sick"* (James 5:14), *"The prayer of faith shall save the sick, and the Lord shall raise him up"* (v. 15), *you like Noah are informed by God, "of things not seen yet,"* and your move is the same as Noah's which is to believe and act accordingly.

Note: Fallen nature is governed by what it senses; but faith is governed by the pure <u>WORD</u> of God, and is nothing less than expecting God to do what He promises - treating Him like an honest Being.

1. Faith never waits to see before believing.
2. Faith <u>knows</u> God has spoken truth and doesn't lie.
3. Faith blows the ram's horn before the walls fall.
4. Faith never judges by senses (symptoms).
5. Faith rests on the solid ground - the pure Word of God.
6. Faith expects what God promised.

7. We know the symptoms that make us doubt are "lying vanities" (Jonah 2:8).
8. We know God is "plenteous in mercy" Psalms 86:5.
9. We must cooperate with God and His Word, by <u>not</u> being occupied by what the devil says.
10. There are two different types of healing.
    i. *"They shall recover"* is one (Mark 16:18).
    ii. Instant healings are working miracles (1 Corinthians 12:9).
11. We know God's Word is settled in heaven (Psalms 119:89).

God's compassionate heart yearns to heal us more than we have the capacity to desire it; but we keep Him waiting until we have the *"faith that cometh by hearing" (Rom. 19:17)*, and act on that faith, because God will not cheat and move out of turn. When God's Word <u>alone</u> is our reason for believing, our prayer is answered before we see or feel it. This is faith!

Remember the order of healing: faith, fact, then the healing feeling. 1 Thessalonians 2:13. When we act out of "full assurance" (Hebrews 10:22) God begins to heal.

Jonah inside the fish did act out his faith by saying *"I will sacrifice unto thee with the voice of thanksgiving" (Jonah 2:9)*. Acting on our faith by praising and thanking God in advance, is shown throughout history to be, His appointed way for appropriating His blessings (Hebrews 13:15).[6]

APPLICATION

When Appropriating Your Bodily Healing Make Satan Listen to Your Praise

Don't listen to the father of lies!
Make him listen to your praising God for His promise!
(Psalm 150:6) (John 14:1, 27) (Philippians 4:6) (I Peter 5:7).
Real faith rejoices in the promises of God as if it had already experienced the deliverance and was enjoying it.
When coming to God for salvation or healing, it is essential for each one to decide whether he shall allow the hiss of the serpent to rise above the voice of God.
When you've been anointed for healing, Satan tells you that you will not recover, say to him;
"It is written" (Matt. 4: 4-10).
Yes, *"It is written."* they shall recover.
Reading Mark 16:18, *"They shall take up serpents; and they if they drink any deadly thing, it shall not hurt them; they shall lay hands on the sick, and they shall recover."*
James 5:15 says, *"The Lord shall raise him up."* That means it is as if the Lord Himself anointed you, then anointed him
(the one you are praying for) with oil in the name of the Lord.
Expect Him to honor His promise.
James 4:7 says *"Submit to God"* first then *"Resist the devil"*.
Whenever we are affected by any other voice more than the voice of God, we have forsaken the Lord's way for our healing.
The basis for our faith is the Lord's compassion! To believe without doubt that Christ's words "It is finished" are a literal statement of an unchangeable fact invariably brings deliverance.
Let us stand on His promise and "blow the ram's horn" of faith and thanksgiving until the walls of affliction fall down flat.
Faith doesn't wait for the walls to fall down, faith shouts them down!
"Same O" FF Bosworth was a mighty man of God.
He lived from 1877 – 1958.

XXIII
Paul's Thorn

"And lest I should be exalted above measure through the abundance of the revelations, a thorn in the flesh was given to me, a messenger of Satan to buffet me, lest I be exalted above measure. Concerning this thing I pleaded with the Lord three times that it might depart from me. And He said to me, 'My grace is sufficient for you, for My strength is made perfect in weakness'. Therefore mostly I will rather boast in my infirmities, that the power of Christ may rest upon me. Therefore I take pleasure in infirmities, in reproaches, in needs, in persecutions, in distresses for Christ's sake: for when I am weak, then am I strong."

2 Corinthians 12: 7-10

Paul's "thorn in the flesh" has led to absurd <u>wrong</u>, widespread teachings:

- God is the author of disease.
- God desires some of His most devout children to remain sick.
- That Paul had eyes filled with unspeakable pus.
- That Jesus Christ gave this eye disease to Paul.
- That "My grace is sufficient for thee." meant it was better for Paul to be sick than well.
- That "thorn" was a bodily affliction.

The "thorn in the flesh" scripture plainly states the Canaanites would be a constant annoyance to Israel. Josh. 23:13 says, *"know for certain that the Lord your God will no longer drive out these nations from before you. But they shall be snares and traps to you, and scourges on your sides and thorns in your eyes, until you perish from this good land which the Lord your God has given you."* 2 Sam. 23:6 says, *"But the sons of rebellion shall all be as thorns thrust away, Because they cannot be taken with hands."* The thorn was *"the messenger of Satan".* 2 Corinthians 12:7 says, *"And lest I should be exalted above measure by the abundance of the revelations, a thorn in the flesh was given to me, a messenger of Satan to buffet me. Least I be exalted above measure."* It is an angel. Matt.25:41 says, *"Then He will also say to those on the left hand. Depart from Me, you cursed, into the everlasting fire prepared for the devil and his angels."* Or you might say a messenger, or not a disease.

Paul's thorn was an angel of Satan that came "to buffet me". "Buffet" means "blow after blow" (Mark 4:37) (Mark 14:65). Paul's thorn was, as he himself plainly showed, a satanic personality and not a disease!

In Acts 9:16 God said to Ananias, *"I will show him how great things he must suffer for my name's sake"* - not by sickness, but by the persecutions that Paul enumerated as his buffetings in 2 Cor. 12:10. Infirmities in that verse is to make every Christian realize his weakness and inability in his own strength and then stand up against a satanic messenger and pass triumphantly through! Paul saw the grace of God was sufficient to strengthen him through "reproaches", "persecutions" etc. That's why he no longer asked for it to be removed! His buffetings are enumerated in First and Second Corinthian are plainly to be seen. In enumerating them we see that Paul mentioned almost everything that one could think of except sickness or ophthalmic disease.

Widespread perversion of the Scriptures dealing with Paul's thorn in the flesh is inspired by Satan, because it gets him the privilege of carrying on his evil work of afflicting and tormenting the bodies of humanity. Why don't the people - that teach Paul was to glory in his sickness, glory in their sicknesses, instead of trying to get rid of them. It says in second Corinthians 12:7 that the buffetings were there lest he should be exalted above measure. Paul wrote the greater portion of the New Covenant. The scripture shows his thorn did not hinder him from laboring "more abundantly" than all others. In 1 Corinthians 15:10 it says, *"But by the grace of God I am what I am, and His grace toward me was not in vain; but I labored more abundantly than they all, yet not I, but the grace of God which was with me."* We are to be prepared for "every good work" (2 Timothy 2:21). Confined to a sickroom by a "thorn in the flesh" you cannot "abound to every good work" (2 Corinthians 9:8). Paul taught in 2 Corinthians 1:20 that a promise of God, included all His promises to heal, owe their existence and power to the substitutionary work of Christ for us, and that the redeeming work of Christ was for all.

Paul differentiated between miracles and healing. He did not believe every person would instantly be made whole. Neither Trophemus sick at Miletum (2 Timothy 4:20), and Epaphroditus was *"sick nigh unto death"* (Phil. 2:27) - they didn't recover instantaneously (vv. 25-30). Paul believed the sick themselves had to have faith for healing. Acts 14:9-10 says, *"The man heard Paul speaking, Paul, observing him intently and seeing that he had faith to be healed, said with a loud voice, 'Stand up straight on your feet!' And he leaped and walked."* In Mark 6:1-6 we see where Jesus Himself could do no miracle in Nazareth because of community unbelief.[1]

God's covenant of healing is established in "the church" for today. Glory in the TRUTH that the fact Healing is ours, and can be appropriated by a living faith in the pure Word of God.

APPLICATION

Believe it, it is truth.

FF Bosworth is way out of my league. But, spirit to spirit I know he is right on target with his teachings! He is one to whom we can learn much by his life of victories, "Same O."

Ask the Holy Spirit to bring greater understanding
and revelation to your mind and heart.
Remember "Same O." God does not have favorites.

XXIV
Angels - Heaven's Host

When we study angels, we must not let our avalanche of angel-ology lead us astray. The Holy Bible is our <u>only</u> reliable source. The word angel appears in the Bible 300 times. The Gallop poll of 1996 said that 7 out of 10 Americans believe in angels. That's the good news. The bad news is 50% of the seven only believe in "good angels". They don't believe in evil angelic hosts. This shows much ignorance about angels. However, the proliferation of literature about angels and demons and the realm of the spirit they inhabit reveals most everyone, religious or not, is definitely fascinated with the super natural. "Same-O", are you fascinated with these spiritual beings? We are in the final days of this age, called "the church age", or the "dispensation of Grace" or "the dispensation of the Acts of the Holy Spirit". So where is this taking us? Let's look at some history.

In 70 A.D. the Roman emperor leveled Jerusalem and massacred "the church". We find for 1900 years the Jews had no homeland. In 1948 Israel was recognized as a nation, and Jews from all over the world began to return to their homeland, and still are returning to this day. Jesus said in Mark 13:30 that the generation witnessing this regathering of Israel won't die: *"Verily I say unto you, that this generation shall not pass, till all these things be done."* <u>We</u> are that generation! We are living in "that day" when Jesus is about to set up His earthly reign!

When learning about angels we must discern the difference between the spiritual realm and our natural senses. I am using the Word of God to lead us on this journey, not the worldly, carnal mind of man. Let's find out what we can learn about angels to understand their ministry.

Yes, I believe we are the generation to see the close of this age and will witness the establishment of Jesus' millennial reign. In *"that day"* God will bring His kingdom, the realm of the Spirit, into contact with the natural temporal earth. Yes, Jesus sets up his earthly kingdom in Israel.

Some day we, who are born again, will reign with Jesus and judge the angels. First Corinthians 6:3 says, *"Do you not know that we shall judge angels? How much more, things that pertain to this life?"* But for now let's keep our attention in this era, not the hereafter. Hebrews 1:14 identifies the angels as *"ministering spirits, sent forth to minister for them who shall be heirs of salvation".* Angels have one purpose; they are sent forth to minister to the heirs of salvation, both in this present time and in the eternal hereafter. Remember, we are the ones who have been made a little lower than God, in His image, and He has put all things under our feet. In God's creative order we are second behind God the Father, God the Son, and God the Holy Ghost. We are created to rule with Him.[1]

Exodus 23:20 shows us that God intended the ministry of angels to be something more than a mere "safety net" for us when we begin sinking in our circumstances.[2] Hebrews 13:8 tells us, Jesus is the same yesterday, today, and forever. When we were created God had a specific safe path for us and he sends angels to bring us into the destiny He has prepared. Psalms 34:7 says, *"The angel of the Lord encampeth round them that fear him, and delivereth them"* KJV. In every area of our life God has commissioned angels to go before us to prepare the way. We are to commission our angels on a daily basis. We can't just "boss" our angelic host around. The angels listen and get instruction from God on our behalf. When our words line up with God our angels get very busy.

First we must make a distinction between the natural world and the world of the Spirit.

Hebrews 2:1 says, *"Therefore we must give the more earnest heed to the things we have heard, lest we drift away."* KJV

Colossians 3:2 says *"Set your mind on things above, not on things on the earth." KJV*

Colossians 2:17-18 *"Which are a shadow of things to come, but the substance is of Christ. Let no one cheat you of your reward, taking delight in false humility and worship of angels, intruding into those things which he has not seen, vainly puffed up by his fleshly mind,..." KJV*

We must give attention to the unseen realm because it supersedes this temporal world. We have been taught to rely upon our five senses and our natural abilities to make decisions. It is a major adjustment to base your life on the unseen realm! It takes developing our sixth sense of faith to move in the spirit realm.

Jesus spoke of angels in His ministry. John 1:51 says, *"Jesus said, Verily, verily, I say unto you, Hereafter ye shall see heaven open, and the angels of God ascending and descending upon the Son of man".* This depicts angels going up and coming down - heavenly beings going back and forth ministering to the heirs of salvation. Jesus in Matthew 26:53 says, *"Or do you think that I cannot now pray to My Father, and He will provide Me with more than twelve legions of angels?"* if He actually needed them. If He can summon twelve legions of angels to come to His aid, WE CAN TOO! This is a part of God's supernatural provision provided in the Atonement for us, as Born-Again Believers. The angels are sent to deliver us from the judgment that is already on the earth because of sin. We must respond correctly to them.

The assistance of angels is a blessing, but we aren't to live only by the ministry of them. *"...The just shall live by faith..." Hebrews 10:38*. We are what we believe! We must cultivate our lives by the <u>fullness</u> of God's Word. John 1:16 says, *"And of His fullness we have all received, and grace for grace."* Proverbs 23:7 says, *"For as he thinks in his heart so is he."* Not just the angel aspect!

We have a lot we can learn from Elisha. "Same O" read in 2 Kings 6:8-10, 11-15, 16-17, and find the story about Elisha and his servant being totally surrounded by the Syrian soldiers. Syria was going to kill Elisha for his foretelling to Israel's king the enemy's plans. The

Syrian king finally found out it was Elisha "the man of God" who was giving away his secrets. As Elisha's servant woke up one morning he looked into the natural world and saw himself and Elisha as "dead meat", because they were surrounded by the enemy. Elisha prayed for his servant to see into the spirit realm what Elisha could see, for Elisha knew the unseen realm supersedes the temporal world. Elisha wasn't fearful. He didn't rely strictly on the natural realm of seeing with his eyes.

Did you know we can develop our sixth sense, (which is faith), using our spiritual eyes and ears. We do this by focusing on the spiritual realm? Perhaps you'll see an angel or two before finishing your walk on earth. In reality everybody responds to the spiritual realm in one way or another.

<u>First response</u>: The Syrian King denied the spiritual realm. Today natural-minded people see no other way but their thought process or their way.

<u>Second response</u>: Elisha's servant allowed fear to rise up and he desired to flee. He had <u>no</u> natural hope of survival.

<u>Third response</u>: The Syrian King after learning "the man of God: was working in an unseen realm - wanted to catch him. (Note: The king knew God was telling Elisha what he needed to win the war. Why didn't that occur to the king? Elisha could hear his plans of making a capture.) Born-again believers make this same mistake. People see that the real challenges in their lives come from the unseen realm, yet they are still trying to meet those challenges by applying natural solutions!

<u>Fourth response</u>: Elisha's response is the correct one to the problem. He relied TOTALLY on the resources and power of the unseen realm. Then Elisha prayed, *"Lord, I pray thee, open his eyes (servant's), that he may see (2 Kings 6:17).* Notice-one panicked, one prayed.

Prayer opens you to the reality of the unseen realm. You must have a vital prayer life to appropriate "the ministering angels." Some prayers don't work because you ask and consume it upon your lust, James 4:2, 3!

Please remember John 14:3 for it says, *"Whatsoever ye shall ask in <u>my name</u> (Jesus' name) that will I do."*

Elisha looked to God through prayer and was continuously delivered.[3] We, too, can receive the angelic deliverance of God by <u>not</u> relying upon the natural, but on GOD!

We must first be fully aware of the presence and activity of the unseen realm of the spirit and then we must be aware of <u>speaking the right words.</u> "Same O", do you believe our words control our believing, our thinking, our behavior and even the direction our lives will take (James 3:3-5)? Words make us or break us. We learned in the chapter on WORDS that Proverbs 18:21 says, *"Death and life <u>are</u> in the power of the tongue."* We must understand the powerful relationship of our words to the angelic realm. Psalm 103:20, 21 says, *"Bless the Lord you His angels, Who excel in strength, <u>who do His word</u>, <u>Heeding the voice of His word.</u> Bless the Lord, all you His hosts, You ministers of His, who do His pleasure."* God's angels do his pleasure, God doesn't do any dirty work! If you want the angels to have something to work with, you have to put voice to the Word of God. Don't put voice to fear and unbelief.[4] That is important "Same O."

APPLICATION

Mac Hammond says there are five levels of words that have a bearing on the spiritual realm of our angels. Our words impact virtually every aspect of who we are and the quality of life we presently experience.

First Level: WORD OF LIFE
If we are a doer of the word (James 1:22), we speak the word and order our life. Thus, we loose the ministering spirits to do His pleasure, which is to prosper us.

Second Level: VOCABULARY OF SILENCE
If you can't put voice to God's Word, just say nothing at all.
Even as in Joshua 6:3-5 where the Israelites were to march around Jericho, Joshua said in 6:10 to be quiet, don't talk.
He knew they were whiners!
Today if you can't speak the words, just keep quiet and keep putting the Word into your heart.

Third Level: WATCH OUT FOR IDLE WORDS
Idle words produce nonproductive behavior.
Matthew 12:36 says *"Every idle word that men speak, they shall give account thereof in the day of judgment."*

Fourth Level: DON'T MURMUR AND COMPLAIN
Here you are lower on the scale from life to death.
1 Corinthians 10:10 says *"Neither murmur ye, as some of them also murmured and were destroyed of the destroyer."* KJV.
Think about the Israelites who died in the wilderness for murmuring.
They are our example to make sure we don't grumble, complain, and murmur.
The blessings of God will forever escape you by these wrong words.

Fifth Level: DANGEROUS WORDS
Avoid this one with a passion.
They are words totally contrary to the Word of God
and the words of life.[5]

There are two kinds of angels out there:
the good and godly angelic host who hearken to the voice of God's Word;
and the others who are fallen angels, but they too respond to words.
When you speak contrary to the Word of God you have disabled your ministering angels and have commissioned the angelic host of darkness to do in your life what they know - steal, kill, and destroy (John 10:10).
Give proper guard to the words of your mouth "Same O" and the "ministry of angels" will become an active factor in your life - with blessings and favor.
Believe the spirit realm is a reality.
Believe your words create your tomorrows, because they do.
When you speak contrary to God's instructions in the Holy Bible you reap what you sow - destruction.
When you love Jesus and speak the rules of "life" you'll walk through trials into victory, for your angels will work it for you.
Angels move upon the spoken Word of God, for people that have a covenant relationship with Him.
Make sure you are in covenant with God. If you are questioning your relationship with God refer back to chapter four for help.
Remember you must develop a loving relationship with your Redeemer by reading and meditating on His Word and developing your prayer life.
Refer back to chapters seventeen and nineteen to line up with His "Kingdom Rules".
There is a place God has planned for each of us, a divinely appointed destiny that flows with milk and honey.

We need to renew our mind and heart and actions to the instructions given by God.
So clean up your words "Same O" and "... *seek first the kingdom of God and His righteousness, and all these things shall be added to you."* Matthew 6:33.

XXV
Abundant Life

Salvation is not just to get saved to escape the fires of hell (Revelation 20:14-15), but to get to know God the Father, Jesus and the Holy Spirit. We need a firsthand relationship with them! It takes time and discipline to develop a relationship. "Same O" it was way back in the early eighties when I sought out God asking him, "What is it to walk in the abundant life." I learned an abundant life is a Spirit-Filled life and the benefits of an abundant life are all received by faith. Over the years I learned it involves:

- Reading and meditating on the Word expecting to hear God's voice
- Learning to pray with my known tongue as well with my unknown language of the Holy Ghost
- Learning to find the promise that is needed for a victory in order to have a breakthrough
- Learning to stand in faith while speaking the word for victory long before a victory manifests
- Using "His Name" in authority to combat the enemy that comes against a born again person
- Learning who I am "in Christ" and walking it out with joy unspeakable
- And much more...

Abundant life comes as a person is obedient to God's Word. Yes, "Same O", we must learn His kingdom rules and follow them with the love and compassion He has given to us. One "kingdom rule" or spiritual law of faith is: "The union of our hearts and wills with God's will and purpose, and where this unity is lacking results are impossible."[1] Think about that statement, and its ramifications "Same O." God does not expect all of us to be preachers or missionaries in foreign lands. He wants us to know Him so we can know His destiny for us. He has planned a special destiny for each of us to walk out with joy. When walking in our God given destiny, we find it to be our promised land, a land of milk and honey in the here and now-today!! God's destiny for each of us is to "do that job" with God at the helm. Our job could be as a carpenter, farmer, CEO, astronaut, preacher, etc., but we are to let God be the Master of it all. How to live the abundant life is no secret: it is revealed in our Lord and Savior Jesus Christ, *"...in that he died, he died unto sin once for all; but the life he lives, He lives to God.: (Romans 6:10).* We each need to work our "job" and truly let God live through us, too. Faith that saves identifies you with Christ in his death – this is eternal life. Faith that yields identifies you with Christ in His resurrection – this is abundant life. It is one thing to have eternal life by faith, it is quite another thing to have abundant life by faith. It is one thing for you to be "made the righteousness of God in him" (2 Corinthians 5:21); it is another thing for you to realize His righteous life is in you (1 John 3:7). It is one thing for you to live in Christ (2 Corinthians 5:17); it is another thing for Christ to live His life through you (Colossians 1:27).

We, the Believer have a choice. "Same O" we can yield unto God by faith and enjoy abundant life, or we can yield unto sin and endure a defeated life (Revelation 3:1). God would have you know the power of a yielded life; it will lift you above circumstances that circumvent abundant living. The abundant life begins when you yield to Him as Master, allowing Him to live His life through you by faith. (Paraphrased from the KJV page 1060 footnote 1).[2]

So to have victories in our walk we must realize forgiveness is top priority (Matthew 6:14). Forgiveness must be given to others, and yourself, as well as forgiving God as you finally surrender to the fact that 'His Way' is always right. Yes, forgiveness is at the top of the list and will bring great peace (from the Prince of Peace) with harmony for your soul!

To have victories we must realize what we have "IN MY NAME." John 14:13, 14 says, *"And whatever you shall ask in my name, that will I do, that the Father may be glorified in the Son."* Remember the word "ask" in the Greek means "demands." "You are not demanding it of God. You are demanding that force, that are injurious shall be broken, that diseases shall be healed, that circumstances shall be changed, that money shall come.[3] That, "Same O" is our legal right as a member of God's family. Notice this Covenant of ours guarantees to us physical protection... protection from the enemy, from pestilence and from disease. That in a nut shell "Same O" is our eternal life - not death; it is our health - not sickness, and our prosperity not lack.

Talking about prosperity 3 John 2 says, *"Beloved I pray that you may prosper in all things and be in health, just as your soul (mind, will, emotions) prospers."* God wants to prosper you, but our question is how? Will he give you a money tree? No. He will do it by prospering your soul. He'll plant the seeds of prosperity in your mind.

Think about Joseph in Genesis 39. Joseph was sold as a slave to the Egyptians. He didn't have any money or freedom. God gave Joseph great wisdom and the ability he needed to help his master prosper. Joseph was put in charge over all the Pharaoh's possessions.

At that point Joseph ended up in prison because of a lie. We find God gave Joseph insight no other man in Egypt had. Joseph thus became an honored man of respect and leadership. Joseph became the top CEO of all the food in the country! You see no matter how bad a situation becomes God can reveal spiritual secrets that open doors to success. This works anywhere and everywhere "Same O."

We are to get out from under! 1 John 4:4 says, *"You are of God, little children, and have overcome them because He who is in you is greater that he who is in the world."* God says we do not have any business letting problems and situations rule over us. Think about Joseph "Same O." We need to cooperate with God's kingdom rules (laws) to receive His abundant life. Joseph did!

Going back to being righteous in God and knowing that I am the righteousness of God should put a nail in coffin of guilt and condemnation that plays in our minds! Joseph did not let bitter emotions rule him, he kept his eyes and thoughts on his God! Romans 4:13 says, *"For the promise that he would be the heir of the world was not to Abraham or to his seed through the law, but through the righteousness of faith."* We all have a "self" that lets circumstances dominate us and causes us to be powerless or we can choose to go the other direction. We can choose and learn to think on things above, things that God through Christ Jesus has paid for with his blood on Calvary. We can call things that are not (Romans 4:17) until they manifest, because they are paid for by Jesus. Remember these things "called for" must line up with His word in the first place.

"Same O" are you keenly aware that financial lack is a curse from the enemy. The bible says the curse is a destructive force. In Deuteronomy 28 we find listed the blessings (prosperity) from verses 1-14. In verses 15-31 we find the curses as described by God. We who are born again are redeemed from the curse (Galatians 3:13). We can line up our thinking, and our minds, with the TRUTH of God's Word, and thus our lives won't have to live under this curse or lack.

We must remember to recall what is ours. We should remind ourselves of God's faithfulness, his compassion for us and that his mercies are new every morning. I like to remind myself of Psalm 103:1-17.

- He forgives all my sins
- He heals all my diseases
- He crowns me with loving-kindness and tender mercies
- He satisfies my mouth with good things so my youth is renewed like the eagles
- He (I like this one "Same O".) executes righteousness and judgment for you against oppression
- He sets you free

- He makes known His ways to you - wonderful, wonderful, "Same O."
- He gave you His grace and mercy in times of need.

This is special, we need to remember these are ours every day and look for them to happen in our daily walk as we are led by the Holy Spirit. Philippians 3:20 says, *"For our citizenship is in heaven, from which we also eagerly wait for the Savior, the Lord Jesus Christ."* Remember this, our citizenship is in God's kingdom and his kingdom rules are different from the natural man's world's rules, who has **not** been adopted into God's kingdom.

APPLICATION

Man succeeds because he thinks he can.
Man fails because he believes he will.
Proverbs 23:7 says, *"For as he thinks in his heart, so is he..."*

When dealing with any problem in life,
we must unearth the deepest root. The devil's strategy of
condemnation is perhaps the deepest root
or tactic to destroy the Believer.
This "root" of condemnation exists in the spiritual realm and can be
destroyed by the power of Jesus "finished work."[4]

A vast number of people are not living an abundant life yet they won't
step out of the boat (step out of the natural, step out of what they are
doing that is not working and do something different.)
Fear is part of the factor that holds them back.
We know fear is the opposite of faith.

The abundant life exists in our lives because of our faith walk.
Learn to doubt your doubts and feed your faith.
Doubt is not the enemy of faith. Doubt is the proving ground of faith!!
Use this thought as a check in your spirit to rise above doubt.
In the amplified bible we read, *"I have told you these things so that in Me you may have (perfect) peace and confidence. In the world you have tribulation and trials and distress and frustration, but be of good cheer... I have overcome the world"* (John 16:33).

We must remember we are not just in the world.
We are in Jesus in the world, and that is a big difference!
You are in Him and He's overcome every problem.
We are the overcomer, we aren't defeated trying to get victory.
We have the victory and the Devil is trying to take it away from us.

Satan is doing his best to rob you of your victory
that already belongs to us.

Think about the fact the victorious Jesus lives in you "Same O."
The Anointed one, the glorified and resurrected Lord, the
Ruler of the Universe lives in us! (John 16:15:33).

Yes, we are born-again to victory!

Your invitation to abundant life is found in Isaiah 55:1a, 2b, 3a, and b, it says, *"Listen carefully to Me, and eat what is good, and let your soul delight itself in abundance. Hear and your soul shall live; and I will make an everlasting covenant with you -."*

Jesus is Lord of the heaven and earth, make Him Lord of your life!

XXVI
Trust Me

This title is commanding us to "Trust Him" as we enter the era of dominion linked with Omnipotence; filled with Him who is greater than he that is in the world, with the wisdom of Him, who spoke a universe into being with a legal right to use "His Name" in every crises of our lives.[1] Proverbs 3:5-8 says, *"Trust in the Lord with all your heart, and lean not on your own understanding; in all your ways acknowledge Him, and He shall direct our paths. Do not be wise in your own eyes; Fear the Lord and depart from evil. It will be health to your flesh and strength to your bones."*

Those words are life to us. To trust, really trust, Him means to surrender your will to His will. God is always a Good God. Any crisis (trouble) that happens is because we live in a fleshly body, a fallen world and have an enemy, Satan! But God, yes God is our refuge and rock – we must "Trust Him."

Do we trust Him for the fact that Jesus has paid the price for us to stop being sin-conscious and become Christ-conscious! Yes, we ask for forgiveness and repent, which means turning away from any sin committed as a Believer. Can we "Trust Him" for the fact He paid the price long before this day (5.5.13) and long before we were even born in sin. Turning our face toward Jesus quickly causes us to leap over the negative sin and concentrate on the finished work of Christ. It is ours, we are in Him, and He is in us. John 15:5 says, *"I am the vine you are the branches,*

He who abides in Me, and I in him, bears much fruit; for without Me you can do nothing."

Being Christ-conscious you will have peace with God through our Lord Jesus Christ. We'll trust Him in times of our need instead of blaming Him or running from Him. Romans 8:16 says, *"the Spirit Himself bears witness with our spirit that we are children of God."* Being this child of God we can see a dual picture of ourselves in Mark 10:16 *"He* (Jesus) *took them* (the children) *up in His arms, laid His hands on them, and blessed them."* He has done His part and thrown His arms wide open to us as a child and as an adult. Let us learn to "Trust Him" and believe Him with our lives. May we follow the Holy Spirit's daily leading as we walk out our journey. May we learn to receive His Presence and His Love and "Trust Him!" He would not command us to believe Him with all of our heart, mind, soul and strength if it were not possible!

APPLICATION

TRUST IS WHERE THE RUBBER MEETS THE ROAD "SAME O."

I can't Trust - for you.

God can't Trust - for you.

Your Mom can't Trust - for you.

Nobody can Trust for you – but you.

It is the Holy Spirit that will bring revelation to your inner most being. This revelation is inside of you, in your spirit.
It is stronger than logic or evidence.

When faith is mixed with His Word it will produce
a divine revelation.

So do not ever give up "Same O."
The Holy Spirit is the author and finisher of our faith (Hebrews 12:2).

XXVII
Tell Them I Am Coming

"Now this I say, brethren, that flesh and blood cannot inherit the kingdom of God; nor does corruption inherit incorruption. Behold, I tell you a mystery: We shall not all sleep, but we shall all be changed – in a moment, in the twinkling of an eye, <u>at the last trumpet</u>. For the trumpet will sound, and the dead will be raised incorruptible, and we shall be changed. For this corruptible must put on incorruption, and this mortal must put on immortality. So when this corruptible has put on incorruption, and this mortal has put on immortality, then shall be brought to pass the saying that is written: "Death is swallowed up in victory'."

(1 CORINTHIANS 15:50-54).

The angel will blow the trumpet to announce the return of Jesus. First Thessalonians 4:16-18 says, *"For the Lord Himself will descend from heaven with a shout with the voice of an archangel, and with <u>the trumpet of God</u>. And the dead in Christ will rise first. Then we who are alive and remain shall be caught up together with them in the clouds to meet the Lord in the air, And thus we shall always be with the Lord. Therefore comfort one another with these words."* Jesus the Son of God and the Son of Man has given us all we need to live in the here and now victoriously (2 Peter 1:1-4). He has given mankind all we need to see Him face to face some day (Revelation 22:4). Jesus is a gentlemen and he lets you <u>choose life</u> with Him or death with the chains of hell (2 Peter 2:4).

Eternity is a long time, so choose Jesus (the God with the GOOD NEWS GOSPEL). Ask God to help you choose your final destination correctly.

"Same O" hell is a real place, created for the devil and his co-horts, (Matthew 25:41). Satan enjoys seeing humans fall into hell daily.

Now is the day of salvation (2 Corinthians 6:20), now is the day to get serious! You are only one heartbeat away from heaven or hell.

Jesus is the only God who gave His life on a cruel cross for you because of His Love for you. He did not stop there. He rose from the dead, taking the keys of death and hell from Satan (Revelations 1:18). Then He did some other things. Later he came back to earth. He walked and talked and ate with his disciples before His ascension to His Father in Heaven (Acts 1:9-10). Matthew 28:9, Mark 16:9, Mark 16:12, Luke 24:36-43, John 20:29, and John 21:15 tell you about some of the people he talked to before He left this earth and ascended to His Father. That is not a fairy tale, "Same O!" It happened! God has never broken any promise and never will (Psalm 89:34). From this you <u>can know</u> he is coming back!

He will not only rapture his children (His Church), but will then set up his kingdom over in Israel (1 Thessalonians 4:16-18). We must believe in Him. We must choose Him by faith into our hearts and lives (Acts 3:21, Acts 4:12).

He's Coming Back,
He said so (Revelation 22:20)!
He doesn't lie (Titus 1:2).

He's Coming,
in the Eastern sky (Matthew 24:27).

He's Coming,
calling his bride, the church, to His supper,
"the marriage supper of the Lamb" (Revelation19:6-9).

He's Coming,
look where his feet will first touchdown on the earth (Zechariah 14:4)
it is the same place from which he left (Acts 1:9:12).

He's Coming,
Yes! He is (Revelations 22:7)!

He's Coming,
back soon, get ready for His appearing! (Revelation 22:12).

This is what I was commissioned to tell.
With this told, I am released from this assignment of telling.

"Same O"

Jesus is coming back very soon.

<u>**Now the choice is in your court!!**</u>

Please believe Jesus.

"HE" LOVES YOU.
No matter what

HE "LOVES" YOU.
Unconditionally

HE LOVES "YOU"
Always

"HE LOVES YOU"
And wants you in heaven with Him

OH!
One more thing.

Do it!
Do it now!

Receive "salvation"

Receive the "Holy Spirit and Power"

Develop a "daily relationship" with your Lord

Act your "belief"

Walk and talk in "faith"

Receive "HIS Love"

Depend on the "Holy Spirit as your Helper"

Love Him always!

Never quit!

You the reader would never have gotten to this page if you were not thirsty for more in your life. So, hunger and thirst for more of your Creator. Do not be content on your current path. Go for the gold, the path of excellence found in the life of Jesus of Nazareth. Put the Holy Word of God first. The Bible is Jesus in print.

Jesus's WORD has the power to dissolve
a "same o" "same o" live and
create a better tomorrow.

"BUILDING A NEW TOMORROW" "GOD'S WAY"

<u>promises contentment in Him, for today!</u>

Endnotes

Chapter 1
1 Andrew Wommack, "You've Already God It!" (Harrison House, Tulsa, Oklahoma, 2006), p.119.

Chapter 2
1 Andrew Wommack, "You've Already God It!" (Harrison House, Tulsa, Oklahoma, 2006), p.83.

Chapter 5
1 Author unknown (Neil Anderson does work like this.)

Chapter 6
1 Smith Wigglesworth, "Ever Increasing Faith" (Gospel Publishing House, Springfield, Missouri, 2001), p. 46.

Chapter 7
1 Brian Baker, "The Normal Church" (Holy Fire Publishing, 717Old Trolley Road, atten: Suite 6, Publishing Unit #11 6, Summerville, SC 29485, 2010), p. 44.

2 EW Kenyon, "The Blood Covenant" (Kenyon's Gospel Publishing Society, P.O. Box 973 Lynnwood Washington 98046, 1999), p.5.

3 I bid., p.20.

4 Kenneth and Gloria Copeland, "From Faith to Faith" (Kenneth Copeland Publications Fort Worth, TX 76192-0001, 1992), January 20.

Chapter 8
1   Charles Capps, "Concepts of Faith" (2nd quarter 2013 magazine, Charles Capps Ministries, P.O. Box 69, England, Arkansas 72046-0069,2013), p.9.

2   Ibid., p. 6.

3   Ibid., p. 4.

Chapter 9
1   Stephen M. Miller, "the Complete Guide to the Bible" (Published by Barbour Publishing, Inc., P.O. Box 719, Uhrichsville, Ohio 44683, 2007), ps. 34-35.

Chapter 10
1   Dr. Carl Baugh, STAR paper of Fort Worth TX January1982, awmi.net [Gospel Truths, Christian Philosophy, 2012, week 40 – Friday, October 5th 2012, through week 41 – Monday through Friday October 8th – 12th 2012].

Chapter 14
1   EW Kenyon, "The Blood Covenant" (Kenyon's Gospel Publishing Society, P.O. Box 973, Lynwood, Washington 9846, 1999), ps.28-31.

2   Ibid., ps. 36-43.

Chapter 15
1   EW Kenyon, "The Blood Covenant" (Kenyon's Gospel Publishing Society, P.O. Box 973, Lynwood, Washington 9846, 1999), ps,30-31.

Chapter 16
1 EW Kenyon, "The Blood Covenant" (Kenyon's Gospel Publishing Society, P.O. Box 973, Lynwood, Washington 9846, 1999), ps.28-31.

2 Ibid., ps.30-31.

Chapter 17
1 Andrew Wommack, "A Better Way to Pray" (Harrison House Publishers, P.O. Box 35035, Tulsa, Oklahoma 74153, 2007).

Chapter 18
1 John Juliano on the "Baptism of the Holy Spirit" (free undocumented article).

2 John Hagee, (www.jhm.org).

3 Ibid. John Juliano

4 Ibid. John Juliano

Chapter 20
1 EW Kenyon, "The Blood Covenant" (Kenyon's Gospel Publishing Society, P.O. Box 973, Lynwood, Washington 9846, 1999), p. 52.

Chapter 21
1 Jerry Savelle, "September letter 2013"

2 U.S.A. www.jerrysavelle.org
Jerry Savelle, "September letter 2013" Jerry Savelle Ministries, Crowley, TX.

Chapter 22

1 FF Bosworth, "Christ the Healer" (Whitaker House, 30 Hunt Valley Circle, New Kensington, PA 15068, 2000), p. 38.

2 Andrew Wommack, "You've Already God It!" (Harrison House, Tulsa, Oklahoma, 2006), p. 186.

3 FF Bosworth, "Christ the Healer" (New Kensington, PA: Whitaker House, 2000), p. 93. (Chapters 22 and 23 are a condensation of his thoughts and quotes. He always used the KJV Bible.)

4 Ibid., ps. 99-104.

5 Ibid., ps. 105-110.

6 Ibid., ps. 112-120.

Chapter 23

1 FF Bosworth, "Christ the Healer" (New Kensington, PA: Whitaker House, 2000) ps. 129-148.

Chapter 24

1 Mac Hammond Ministries, "Angels at Your Service" (P.O. Box 29469, Minneapolis, Minnesota 55429-2946), p. 18.

2 Ibid., ps. 47-48.

3 Ibid., ps. 50-57.

4 Ibid., ps. 61-63.

5 Ibid., ps. 73-84.

Chapter 25

1. FF Bosworth, "Christ the Healer" (New Kensington, PA: Whitaker House, 2000), ps. 107-108.

2. KJV, "King James Version" (P.T.L. Club Partner Edition, Thomas Nelson Inc. Publisher Nashville, Tennessee, zip 37214-1000, 1975), 1060 footnote, One.

3. EW Kenyon, "The Blood Covenant" (Kenyon's Gospel Publishing Society, P.O. Box 973, Lynwood, Washington 9846, 1999), p. 64.

4. Joseph Prince, "Destined to Reign" (Published by Harrison House Publisher, P.O. Box 35035, 2007), p. 131.

Chapter 26

1. EW Kenyon, "The Blood Covenant" (Kenyon's Gospel Publishing Society, P.O. Box 973, Lynwood, Washington 9846, 1999), p. 64.

My Personal Notes

Made in the USA
San Bernardino, CA
20 May 2016